MC Global Ministries'
Fellowship Handbook

What We Believe and Why

But if we walk in the light, as he is in the light, we have fellowship with one another, and the blood of Jesus his Son cleanses us from all sin.
1 John 1:7

What We Believe and Why
MC Global Ministries Fellowship Handbook
Copyright © 2023 MC Global Ministries

This literature describes the mission and ministries of Message of the Cross Chapel Fellowship and Message of the Cross Global Ministries. The explanations, information, and contact information is subject to change.

ISBN 978-1-943412-47-1

Published by -
Wilderness Voice Publishing, LLC
Canon City, Colorado USA
www.wvpbooks.com

"A voice crying in the wilderness - proclaiming the good news of the coming Kingdom!"

Contents

Welcome

Our fellowship welcomes you to seriously study our fellowship handbook. The information, Scripture references, policies, and practices described herein covers what we believe and why. If you are led to become a member of our fellowship, you will need to know and understand how we govern ourselves to maintain a safe and healthy congregation. This handbook is the fellowship's main document that is referenced when there are questions, concerns, or potential conflicts of doctrine or standard practices.

Our Mission

MC Global Ministries is the nonprofit Christian corporation that offers to its team members and their families a Chapel Fellowship. In the MC Global bylaws, its Chapel Fellowship is open to likeminded Christians who desire to attend MC Chapel Fellowship. In the bylaws there are provisions for Christians not working for MC Global Ministries to attend this Chapel Fellowship and can become a member of the fellowship.

Thank you for considering Message of the Cross Chapel Fellowship as your fellowship home and ministry family. We are fully aware that finding and committing to a doctrinally sound fellowship is crucial, especially now as the last days of this age unfold.

Yes, we are a last day's ministry offering fellowship to those in our community. MC Chapel Fellowship is not a typical church. You will discover this as you read through this handbook. The founders of MC Global Ministries understand that Christianity and church fellowship will become challenging in these last days leading to Christ's return

During this time, Christ warned that false leaders would come in his name misleading many and that trouble and stress would mount. (Matthew 24: 5.) Further, the Apostle Paul warned that in the last days many Christians would not endure sound doctrine, but rather accumulate for themselves teachers to suit their own agendas and wander off into myths. (See 2 Timothy 4:3-4.)

We want to make sure from the onset that you understand our position on important and often controversial teachings and practices that cause many to become unprepared for these now difficult times. Our charge is to build disciples of Christ who learn to stand on their own two feet of faith and grow into maturity, walking in a sincere and pure devotion to Christ—becoming prepared to be used of God on the day that he acts.

This is our goal: that those whom we fellowship with learn to follow and obey the *true Christ*, rather than follow a leader, a movement, or a denomination. Today, many Christians are deceived into believing in a false Jesus, empowered by a counterfeit spirit, and learning a different gospel than that of Scripture. (See 2 Corinthians 11:1-4.)

At best, the majority in leadership across all denominations teach a watered-down Gospel that leaves out the more difficult but life transforming words of Christ.

Our fellowship is open to likeminded believers who are serious with Christ and who are confident that God has called them to become involved in a work that builds up Christians into the people whom the Holy Spirit can reside.[1] We desire to make known our stance concerning sound doctrine found in Scripture and eliminate any confusion or misunderstanding.

Our approach to fellowship and ministry, including our statement of faith, has been honed and established through years of study, ministry, and insight from the Spirit of God. You are welcome to request further explanation on these established guidelines, fellowship policies, bylaws, and our ministry approach.

However, if you disagree and take on the goal to change our position concerning doctrine, we hold to be sound and Scriptural, this will constitute a breach of fellowship harmony. Further, if you disagree with our bylaws and statement of faith, we earnestly recommend that you find fellowship elsewhere or start your

---

[1] 1 Corinthians 6:19-20: *"Or do you not know that your body is a temple of the Holy Spirit within you, whom you have from God? You are not your own, for you were bought with a price. So glorify God in your body."*

own fellowship, since contesting our doctrinal positions would bring disharmony and schism. If there is an attempt to change our foundational positions through divisiveness or subversion, that type of approach will end in being banned from fellowship.

We hope that any conflicting views on fellowship practices or our corner stone theological positions can be rectified with in-depth explanation and thorough exhortation of Scripture by answering any questions that you may have. So, feel free to ask us to give an account as to why we hold the following doctrines and theological positions so dearly.

Maturity in Christ: As you review this fellowship handbook, please keep in mind that this ministry is geared to challenge, encourage, and strengthen each fellowship team member. Thus, this fellowship can be considered a discipleship learning and training center versus the traditional church operation that usually offers a myriad of ministries, social amenities, and expansive facilities.

To be direct, we are not here to entertain, cajole, entice, sell, or manipulate you into becoming followers of the leadership, while we soak-up your tithes and offerings and build a giant church facility with a smorgasbord of specialty ministries that tickle ears.

Neither should you expect to sit as a spectator and watch others become ministers of the Gospel. All members of the fellowship will be expected to take part in the work of the ministry in one form or another as each becomes prepared and released by the Holy Spirit.

This ministry emphasizes all the teachings of Christ including the harder, gritty, and challenging teachings that far too many ministries, churches, and movements avoid. If you desire to grow up into Christ who is to be our head and truly know Christ in full maturity, then we encourage you to become familiar with this work. We encourage you to prayerfully seek confirmation from the Lord on making MC Chapel Fellowship your fellowship home. (Study Ephesians 4:1-16.)

The Great Commission

Christ commanded, *"Go therefore and make disciples of all nations, baptizing them in the name of the Father and of the Son and of the Holy Spirit, <u>teaching them to observe all that I have commanded you</u>. And behold, I am with you always, to the end of the age"* (Matthew 28:19-20).

Our leadership's main objective in ministry is to continue to grow in the grace and knowledge of our Lord as we lead and mentor others by example, teaching each to observe all that Christ taught.

The sincere believer in Christ is expected to learn how to hear the voice of Christ and be led in all of life by the Holy Spirit, *"For all who are led by the Spirit of God are sons of God"* (Romans 8:14). Further, each must learn how to allow the discipline of the Lord and the leadership of the Holy Spirit to work death to one's carnal nature. *"And those who belong to Christ Jesus have crucified the flesh with its passions and desires"* (Galatians 5:24).

Many Christians become lackadaisical and let (even demand) leadership lead and guide them rather than doing the hard work of true discipleship, where Christ becomes Master and Savior being led by the Holy Spirit. Our mission therefore is to help sincere Christians become sons and daughters of God, learning to be led, in all of life, by the Holy Spirit—for Jesus said, *"My sheep hear my voice, and I know them, and they follow me"* (John 10:27).

To that end, we strive with all the energy, insight, love, and grace that God instills within us, trusting him to add to our ranks good-hearted brethren—in his timing and by his power. *"Him we proclaim, warning everyone and teaching everyone with all wisdom, that we may present everyone mature in Christ. For this I toil, struggling with all his energy that he powerfully works within me"* (Colossians 1:28-29).

As you continue to review this handbook, other aspects of our mission will be explained, helping you decide if this fellowship and ministry training center is the place God wants you to attend and become your fellowship home.

MC Chapel Fellowship – *not a Typical Church*
A Discipleship & Ministry Training Center

Some come to fellowship expecting typical church programs and amenities, where a believer can enjoy a well-rounded diet of entertaining messages, events, and plenty of options in ministry programs to suit a variety of special interests.

Those who have children may also expect typical church services where nursery, daycare, and Sunday school are provided along with teen ministries. These programs and services may be appropriate in a typical church setting but are not part of MC Chapel Fellowship for several reasons. (However, as we grow in resources and facilities, we will provide nursery and other childcare, teen growth ministries, and single parent support programs.)

We believe those attending need to focus on sound doctrine and learn how to be trained and equipped in the day-to-day discipline of the Lord. Those attending who do have children will be encouraged and aided in learning how to raise their children, in the discipline and instruction of the Lord. Each parent is to lead, teach, and encourage his or her children by *example living* in conjunction with routine and specific instruction. (See Ephesians 6:1-4.)

Unfortunately, throughout most denominations, this all-important parental ministry has been carelessly assigned to church staff professionals or volunteers who try their best, but so often have their lessons undermined by parental hypocrisy and laziness. This system of surrogate religious instruction more often splits families rather than facilitate solid parent-child bonding in Christ.

Sunday Home-Schooling: At MC Chapel Fellowship parents learn to *home school* their children concerning the Gospel, sound doctrine, and growth in Christ. Most importantly, parents learn the importance of *example living* to reinforce their lesson plans in the Gospel.

The sincere believer attending our fellowship receives sound instruction on becoming a disciple of Jesus Christ, learning to discern the false and avoid following glorified leaders who are often in reality, wolves out for their own gain. (See Acts 20:29-31.)

Theology that Facilitates Christ-like Character Transformation and Maturity

Studies show that most pastors and ministers are not equipped to meet the demands of ministry. Stress from long hours and the constant demands of life take their toll early for the majority of those called into ministry. The high failure percentages in these studies do not take into consideration people entering the ministry as a profession, who were not called to do so by the Holy Spirit.

Regardless, if called of God or not, most in ministry lack skills in dealing with the carnal Christian they are caring for and lack ability to discern and deal appropriately with evil people hidden in their congregation.

In addition, many in leadership suffer from their own inner issues and defilements from their former life. These issues, along with inadequate salary often strain their marriage. This sorrowful condition primarily stems from lack of knowledge and wisdom due to inadequate curriculum in Bible College and Seminary. [2]

Our ministry leadership concentrates on the study of Scripture and the Holy Spirit's leadership in a practical manner. Our theology is the study of Christ's words [all that he gave as recorded in Scripture] and obedience to his teachings. The following passage is God's answer to the terrible condition church leadership has fallen to in this hour.

"Everyone then who hears these words of mine and does them will be like a wise man who built his house on the rock. And the rain fell, and the floods came, and the winds blew and beat on that house, but it did not fall, because it had been founded on

---

[2] Surveys of pastors conducted from 1989 to 2006 by the Francis A. Schaeffer Institute of Church Leadership Development, Barna, Focus on the Family, and Fuller Seminary shed insight concerning these troubling statistics. The results of these surveys posted on the following websites provide overwhelming data that point to false doctrine, inadequate training, and poor leadership mentoring as the main reasons for Christianity's leadership crisis: churchleadership.org; barna.org; barnabasministriesinc.org.

the rock. And everyone who hears these words of mine and does not do them will be like a foolish man who built his house on the sand. And the rain fell, and the floods came, and the winds blew and beat against that house, and it fell, and great was the fall of it." (Matthew 7:24-27).

The harder, gritty, and life changing words of Christ are now virtually ignored in the formal education curriculum of Christian higher education. Christian literature by popular authors has tried to fill this vacuum of practical life changing theological principles, only to provide quick fix shortcut teachings that make the situation worse in the long run.

Our theology is the serious study of all that Christ commands and teachings in Scripture. Those in leadership must bear fruit of hearing, properly comprehending and doing all of Christ's words and submitting to Christ's lordship and discipline in everyday life.

This is how Christ trained the original disciples and this how the Lord continues to work in raising up true leadership and preparing them to be his servants.

Why the name 'Message of the Cross'

Jesus said to all who followed him, *"If anyone would come after me, let him deny himself and <u>take up his cross daily</u> and follow me. For whoever would save his life will lose it, but whoever loses his life for my sake will save it. For what does it profit a man if he gains the whole world and loses or forfeits himself?"* (Luke 9:23-25).

The work of the cross in the believer's life is the least taught subject throughout Christianity today. Even though many sects and denominations experience large increases in attendance and popularity (that many call growth and revival); nevertheless, most believers lack the true power and love of God flowing within and through their lives. Thus, most Christians lack the ability to touch the world and God's lost sheep in the pure power of the Holy Spirit.

Few Christians receive sound doctrine pertaining to how the principle of the cross (dying to the old carnal self) are to be applied so that Christ can bring newness of life in the power of God. The disciple who embraces the work of the cross will then naturally impart God's power and love within him or herself to others around them.

It is the poignant message of the cross that must and will be at the forefront once again. As troubles and persecution increase for Christians, the sound doctrines of Scripture and the work of the cross in the believer's life will once again be the church's (the body of Christ) marching orders.

The message of the cross, when it is understood and taught properly, is God's primary principle that transforms the carnal nature of the believer into Christ-like character.

The Apostle Paul described the message or the word of the cross this way, *"For the word [message] of the cross is folly to those who are perishing, but to us who are being saved it is the power of God"* (1 Corinthians 1:18).

When Christ has any group of men and women who truly become his disciples; it is then, they will succeed in growing up into salvation by embracing the message of the cross. The message of the cross is to the central principle of God's practical theology. The death to the carnal life by employing the principle of the cross brings the true power of God daily. A believer can once again move freely in as (living waters) newness of life continues to flow into that believer's life. *"For if we have been united with him in a death like his, we shall certainly be united with him in a resurrection like his"* (Romans 6:5).

It is our theme in fellowship, ministry, and day to day living to follow Christ and let the message of the cross bring death to our carnal life daily. The first century Christians embraced the message of the cross, thus those first followers of Christ were called followers of The Way. That journey makes way for the resurrecting power of Christ to bring newness of life—daily!

We learn to live Christ daily, where it is Christ in us leading and empowering, not us working religiously for him in our carnal strength and carnal energies.[3] MC Global Ministries and its Chapel Fellowship, as a

---

[3] Carnal strength and carnal energy: These are human emotional and spiritual powers derived by one's own intentions or motives of heart and personal spirit. A carnal Christian who lives, works, and serves God in church do so in their own volition and convenience, not in obedience to

people are committed to sacrificial worship by presenting our lives in every way as a living sacrifice unto the Lord. (See Romans 12:1-2.)

Accountability to the Lordship of Christ

We may call Christ Lord; however, the challenge of true discipleship is allowing him to be our Master—in every aspect of living. Many Christians, even those who walk in the so-called gifts have learned to act and talk like a disciple of Christ in many ways, yet they do their "own thing" in ministry and seldom submit to the lordship of Christ (many have never been taught otherwise). Christ said, *"Why do you call me 'Lord, Lord,' and not do what I tell you?"* (Luke 6:46).

Thus, many serve the church, ministry, or missions with selfish motives, often ignorantly rebelling against God's will, his timing, and his purposes. *"Not everyone who says to me, 'Lord, Lord,' will enter the kingdom of heaven, but the one who does the will of my Father who is in heaven. On that day many will say to me, 'Lord, Lord, did we not prophesy in your name, and cast out demons in your name, and do many mighty works in your name?' And then will I declare to them, 'I never knew you; depart from me, you workers of lawlessness.'"* (Matthew 7:21-23).

As true disciples of Christ we must learn to become accountable to the person of Christ which does not mean becoming carnally religious, pious, or putting on a pretense as a self-righteous saint (carnally heavenly high-minded and earthly no-good).

Carnal Christians love carnal church growth methods and work tirelessly for leadership, but never embrace the work of the cross and die to their own carnal energies and desires. Roots of bitter jealousy and selfish ambition often are the driving motives for serving, where serving Christ builds up an insecure ego. Insecurities and false responsibility create hidden pools of energy where false and carnal leaders learn to exploit the naïve or carnal believer who carry these hidden issues. Thus, both leader and follower work tirelessly in the flesh in the name of serving Christ. Multitudes of sincere Christians never rest from their own labors and learn to allow the Holy Spirit to lead and guide. (Hebrews 4:11-13.)

Unfortunately, most popular movements and church growth campaigns teach Christians to harness these pools of carnal energy in working for the church, missions, and evangelism. Here at MCCF we learn to embrace the discipline of the Lord and allow the Word of God to become a tool in the hands of the Holy Spirit, exposing our thoughts and intentions of the heart. We desire to be led by the Holy Spirit in good works, church growth, and in the fellowship "body life" harmoniously. We are careful to avoid popular carnal church growth schemes that harness our carnal energies.

The question we keep before ourselves daily is: "Do people see and meet Jesus within us or are we selling a carnally formed version of Christ—which merely amounts to self-promotion." This will become your daily challenge as well.

Leadership and Accountability

Leading those in our care—leading each towards the fulness of Christ is the overriding objective of all those called and appointed to leadership. Each program, Bible study, ministry engagement, meeting, and fellowship service has the main goal of building believers into disciples of Christ. With the practical result of having all in fellowship learn to be led by the Holy Spirit, where Christ is head or leader of all.

Leadership as well as the saints in ministry are to strive for the person of Christ to become head of all. Therefore, leaders, Christian workers, and fellowship attendees are held accountable to the Lordship of Christ.

Leadership at MC Chapel Fellowship is accountable to the Lord to lead and care for those in fellowship—that each obtain the grace of God and for each strive and arrive at state of everyday living where Christ is Lord, and the Holy Spirit leads and guides. We each learn to rest in the Lord's guidance and leadership and cease from being driven by our own carnal energies and self-centered motives.

---

the will and leading of the Holy Spirit; thus, many carnal Christians wreck their own genuine faith and become false Christians, just as the Apostle Paul wrote of these, *"For such persons do not serve our Lord Christ, but their own appetites"* (Romans 16:18).

The MC Global Ministries bylaws incorporate internal accountability between the founding Board of Directors, Corporate Officers, Senior Pastor, Associate Pastors, Staff Pastors, Fellowship Elders, Ministry Team Leaders, and Chapel Fellowship team members.

New Believers and Maturity
Growing Up into Salvation and Coming Away

Becoming a Christian is often referred to as becoming born again, a term that is based on Christ's words: *"Truly, truly, I say to you, unless one is born again he cannot see the kingdom of God…Truly, truly, I say to you, unless one is born of water and the Spirit, he cannot enter the kingdom of God. That which is born of the flesh is flesh, and that which is born of the Spirit is spirit"* (John 3:3-6).

Becoming a true Christian requires a valid encounter with the Holy Spirit which is evidenced by a deep revelation within the heart that Jesus Christ is the one and only Savior and Lord. Along with this there should come a genuine contriteness or grieving over one's sins (past and current) repentance (turning away) and a desire to obey Christ's commends and live a godly life. Then within a short time there should be a desire to know Christ in a deeper way by reading Scripture and by developing a lifestyle of prayer and proper fellowship with likeminded Christians.

The truly born-again Christian is exhorted in Scripture to grow up into salvation and become mature in Christ in every way. (See 1 Peter 2:2 and Ephesians 4:15-16.) In Hebrews we are challenged to move on from the elementary doctrines of Christ and go on to maturity. Repeatedly hearing the basics of salvation and the elementary principles of the Gospel has put many Christians at risk by keeping them naïve, weak, and immature.

This is the primary reason why many new and old Christians alike are vulnerable to false teachers, false teachings, and are easy prey for Satan and his schemes. *"Let us leave the elementary doctrine of Christ and go on to maturity, not laying again a foundation of repentance from dead works and of faith toward God"* (Hebrews 6:1).

Our fellowship concentrates on facilitating true maturity in Christ for each person so that the body life of the fellowship grows in a healthy loving manner, where Christlike character is developed, honed, and humbly exemplified.

The key to obtaining this level of maturity is learning how to embrace sound doctrine, discern the false and the evil, and come away from the false, giving up love for the things of this world and its influences. The sincere Christian who attends MCCF can expect to be encouraged, challenged, and strengthened to succeed in dying to the works of the flesh, no longer being influenced by the worldly and dark-deceptive powers of this present age.

Following Christ is not a magic journey where God whisks believers into a paradise on earth. Rather, Jesus informed the crowds coming to him saying, *"Enter by the narrow gate. For the gate is wide and the way is easy that leads to destruction, and those who enter by it are many. For the gate is narrow and the way is hard that leads to life, and those who find it are few"* (Matthew 7:13-14).

The abundant life that Christ offers is often contrary to happiness that the world offers, which often comes in the form of material blessings, sensual and emotional bliss. However, the life of a true Christian strives for the fullness of God's presence, his joy, his peace, his guidance, his holiness, and his protection. In the original Greek text, this *life* Christ promises is called Zōē life, which is the life we receive from Father God by following Christ and embracing all that our Lord commands.

The following two publications will help both old and new believers gain a deeper understanding on how to walk with Christ in these last days of this age:

- **Equipped for Life and Ministry in the Last Days** *Biblical Principles to help Endure and Minister during the Final Awakening* ISBN 978-1-943412-13-6
- **Crushed in Spirit 2ⁿᵈ Edition** *Help for Christians suffering from a wounded and broken spirit* ISBN 978-1-943412-16-7

Renouncing False Christianity and Spiritualism

Many Christians struggle in their relationship with our heavenly Father and Christ his Son, because of wrong beliefs and misinformation. Studying, understanding, and applying all of Christ's words is vital in establishing one's faith and beliefs in the living God. Jesus warned that many would come in his name to get people to follow them, not follow Christ, for Christ warns, *"See that no one leads you astray. For many will come in my name, saying, 'I am the Christ,' and they will lead many astray"* (Matthew 24:4-5).

There have been many deceitful movements since Christ ascended and left the original Apostles in charge and led by the Holy Spirit. As you grow in the knowledge of God and the Gospel of his Son, you will easily catch wrong teachings, false teachers, and false movements within Christianity. A good resource for further study is a book entitled "Kingdom of the Cults" written by the late Walter Martin.

The following is a short list of false denominations and movements that have strayed from sound doctrine found in properly understanding the word of God. If you have embraced wrong teachings or were attending a Christian "cult" movement, it is important you understand the errors, renounce any latent allegiance, and become cleansed of any defilements such as spiritualism, hypocrisy, or counterfeit gifts.

• Jehovah's Witness and the Watch Tower	• Aryan Nations, Christian Identity Church, Klu Klux Klan, etc.
• Christian Science and New Thought	• United Pentecostal Church
• Mormonism—the Latter-Day Saints	• The Family (Children of God)
• The Church of Scientology	• Roman Catholicism *
• The Twelve Tribes	• Christian Spiritualism**
• Unification Church	• Spiritualism, Astral Projection, Occult ***
• The International Churches of Christ	

*Roman Catholicism: Many reputable theologians regard the Catholic Christian denomination as the most deceptive cult of all. Most of their core beliefs are biblical, but the additional doctrine devised throughout the centuries and embraced by Catholics undermine true faith towards Christ and his Gospel. The list of deceitful and destructive abuses through the years and especially of late demonstrate the abhorrent corruption within Catholicism due to false teachings and its cultish practices. For believers coming to MCCF who have a Catholic background, we recommend the following booklet entitled:

- **Why the Reformation?** *Steps to Recovery for Former Catholics"* ISBN 978-1-943412-44-0

**Christian Spiritualism: Through the years of ministry, counseling, and study of Scripture we have learned that many Charismatic and Pentecostal Christians have become deceived into practicing counterfeit gifts. Unbeknownst to the masses of tongue speaking believers, most have been led to tap into their own personal spirit believing this experience is the baptism of the Holy Spirit. Few discern this error and excel in developing the practice of speaking in tongues as a cure-all for internal issues of the old carnal nature and deliverance from demonic oppression. In reality, a false tongue paves way for counterfeit gifts, as an example the "spirit of divination" posing as the gift of prophesy. We believe in the gifts of the Holy Spirit, but they must be tempered and timed by the discipline and training by the Lord and given according to God's will. This issue will be addressed more thoroughly later in this handbook. Another publication we recommend is the following:

- **The Gift, Gifts, and Fruit of the Holy Spirit** ISBN 978-1-943412-45-7

***Spiritualism, Sorcery, Astral Projection, Paganism, and the Occult: We have found that many new and older Christians who have been involved in biblically forbidden practices and lifestyles prior to their born-again experience and commitment to following Christ still struggle with inner defilements due to those past practices. Renouncing and repenting from such past practices is the first step. *"Also many of those who were now believers* *came, confessing and divulging their practices. And a number of those who had practiced magic arts brought their books together and burned them in the sight of all. And they counted the value of them and found it came to fifty thousand pieces of silver. So the word of the Lord continued to increase and prevail mightily"* (Acts 19:18-20). The second step is to allow the Lord to show you any latent defilements from such past activities. *"Since we have these promises, beloved, let us cleanse ourselves from every defilement of body and spirit, bringing holiness to completion in the fear of God"* (2 Corinthians 7:1). This can be a lifetime process, where these past defiling practices are interwoven and hidden within the one's own old carnal nature and takes time to be brought to light by the Holy Spirit. *"Put off your old self, which belongs to your former manner of life and is corrupt through deceitful desires, and to be renewed in the spirit of your minds, and to put on the new self, created after the likeness of God in true righteousness and holiness"* (Ephesians 4:22-24). An additional resource to assist in becoming cleansed from past defilement:

- **Putting Off the Old—Putting On the New** ISBN 978-1-943412-46-4

Jealousy and Selfish Ambition

In the book of James, we are exhorted to take heed concerning a very insidious condition that can create great difficulties and cause harm to a body of believers in fellowship. *"Who is wise and understanding among you? By his good conduct let him show his works in the meekness of wisdom. But if you have bitter jealousy and selfish ambition in your hearts, do not boast and be false to the truth. This is not the wisdom that comes down from above, but is earthly, unspiritual, demonic. For where jealousy and selfish ambition exist, there will be disorder and every vile practice"* (James 3:13-16).

MCCF members are encouraged to examine inner bitter jealousy and selfish motivation. These two issues of heart can create chaos and relationship problems. Wounded Christian growing up in a dysfunction or abusive home where sibling rivalry or parental favoritism existed are prone to subtly struggle with jealousy and selfish agendas. The disorder and demonic attacks can easily go undetected and eventually lead to serious relationship and fellowship trouble and disharmony.

MCCF leadership pays attention to the red-flag warnings and become trained to confront those who continue to work and live by jealous and selfish motives.

Marriage and Relationships
Christ Centered and Grace Filled

The American culture has changed dramatically over the last sixty years causing instability in marriage, family, and personal relationships. Few are equipped to handle all the accumulated stress from everyday living where spousal relations and family peace and harmony take the brunt of the built-up tension.

What Scripture clearly points out is that these stressors will not subside but continue to increase and eventually become unbearable for the unprepared. The Apostle Paul warned, *"But understand this, that in the last days there will come times of stress. For men will be lovers of self, lovers of money, proud, arrogant, abusive, disobedient to their parents, ungrateful, unholy, inhuman, implacable, slanderers, profligates, fierce, haters of good, treacherous, reckless, swollen with conceit, lovers of pleasure rather than lovers of God, holding the form of religion but denying the power of it. Avoid such people"* (2 Timothy 3:1-5 RSV).

The Gospel of Christ and the New Testament writers lay out sound principles to help us properly deal with strained relationships, dysfunctional family systems, and the pressures of living during an end time culture of sin, anarchy, and chaos. We provide mentoring, counseling, and support for married believers and single parents as well as instruction on maintaining proper relationship boundaries with extended family, co-workers, friends, and singles in dating and importantly proper fellowship boundaries between the brethren.

End of the Age Challenges
You Will Know the Season—Not the Day or Hour!

The many warnings and explanations described by Christ and the Apostles clearly indicate that the end-of-this-age is coming upon us swiftly.

We at MCCF take to heart all that Christ and Scripture describe and warn concerning the coming difficult and even terrible times leading to Christ's appearance.

Jesus warned, *"And there will be signs in sun and moon and stars, and on the earth distress of nations in perplexity because of the roaring of the sea and the waves, people fainting with fear and with foreboding of what is coming on the world. For the powers of the heavens will be shaken. And then they will see the Son of Man coming in a cloud with power and great glory. Now when these things begin to take place, straighten up and raise your heads, because your redemption is drawing near"* (Luke 21:25-28).

Many are recognizing the distress and perplexities; however, through the centuries and especially in the last century, a multitude of false prophets and false alarmists have pronounced coming destruction, the end of the world, and even proclaimed specific dates of Christ's appearance and return. Every date prophesied concerning Christ's return has come and gone leaving many misguided or fanatical Christians looking foolish.

Turned Off, Tuned Out, and in Denial. This and other deceptions have caused naïve and misinformed Christians, as well as unbelievers to be ***turned off*** to the truth of Christ's soon return. Many sincere believers are afraid to examine Scripture for themselves, take a stand on the truth, warn others, and become prepared to endure to the end.

Even as the birth pangs and signs of His coming increase and become obvious to the discerning believer (as clearly recorded in scripture)—few are taking heed. The incessant rise of false alarmists has desensitized many. False prophets, false alarmists, and false teachings inspired by Satan have lulled most Christians to sleep—like the fable of the boy who repeatedly cried "wolf" when none was nearby.

This has caused many to ***tune out*** any doctrinally sound warnings given by genuine messengers who are speaking the truth. Because of this "tuning out," many teachers and pastors refrain from sounding any warning that the end-of-the-age is close at hand.

Then there are the multitudes of deceived believers who have bought into the pre-tribulation rapture fable made popular by such authors as Hal Lindsey in *The Late Great Planet Earth*, and Tim LaHaye and Jerry Jenkins in the *Left Behind* series of books and movies.

Christians who adhere to these false teachings are at great risk of being unprepared to meet Christ and endure the coming severe difficulties. A great number of Christians embrace these contradictions to Christ's own teachings concerning the rapture, causing many to fall into the foolish maiden category as described by Christ in the parable of the Ten Maidens. (See Matthew 25:1-13.)

The Apostle Paul wrote the following warning concerning falling away from embracing sound teachings, *"For the time is coming when people will not endure sound teaching, but having itching ears they will accumulate for themselves teachers to suit their own passions, and will turn away from listening to the truth and wander off into myths"* (2 Timothy 3:3-4).

The pre-tribulation rapture is a myth and millions of Christians are in denial because they believe what they want to believe, not what they should believe based on sound doctrine found in Scripture.[4]

With all these mythical beliefs, a multitude of good-hearted believers are taking it easy and are arrogantly prancing through life in gross ***denial***, believing they are sincerely following Christ.

However, they are not really allowing Christ to discipline and transform their carnal nature—in order that Christ may truly know them and that, they may learn to abide in him. They know of Christ, but Christ

---

[4] Carefully read Christ's explanation of when the rapture occurs in Matthew 24:29-31 and in Mark 13:24-27, in both passages Jesus begins by saying "after that tribulation" is when the rapture will take place.

does not know them. Just as Jesus warned that in the end he would say to many deceived Christians, *"Truly I say to you, I do not know you."*[5]

Few today fear God or desire to embrace the daily work of the cross to become sanctified and transformed—become changed within one's nature (character) to be Christ-like. They do not understand that the Great Tribulation will force the insincere and false believer to either fall away or get it right. This coming trouble will also challenge the true believer to become all the more pure and prepared.

Jesus taught: *"From the fig tree learn its lesson: as soon as its branch becomes tender and puts out its leaves, you know that summer is near. <u>So also, when you see these things taking place, you know that he is near, at the very gates</u>. Truly, I say to you, this generation will not pass away until all these things take place. Heaven and earth will pass away, but my words will not pass away. "<u>But concerning that day or that hour, no one knows,</u> not even the angels in heaven, nor the Son, but only the Father. <u>Be on guard, keep awake</u>. For you do not know when the time will come. It is like a man going on a journey, when he leaves home and puts his servants in charge, each with his work, and commands the doorkeeper to stay awake. Therefore stay awake—for you do not know when the master of the house will come, in the evening, or at midnight, or when the cock crows, or in the morning—lest he come suddenly and find you asleep. And what I say to you I say to all: Stay awake"* (Mark 13:28-37).

Participating in this fellowship and its ministries, you will be encouraged and challenged to wake up and stay awake, consistently praying and becoming prepared for the dark and challenging days that are swiftly coming upon us. Importantly, we look forward to our Savior's appearance, where at the end of the Great Tribulation period Christ will call up the true saint (the rapture), just as the wrath of God falls upon a rebellious and wicked world. (See Matthew 24:29-31; Revelation 6:12-17.)

Preparing for the "Midnight Cry Awakening"

As cited previously, prophesies of Christ and of the Apostles concerning the end-of-this-age are being fulfilled right before our eyes. The birth pangs of the coming kingdom of God, which Jesus spoke of are increasing with intensity and frequency. We will not know the day or hour of Christ's appearance, but Christ expects his servants to know the season and to be ready. Christ clearly says that one must be watching always and diligently praying for strength to endure the last days challenges until he appears.

Far too many church-going Christians have taken it easy like the foolish in many of Christ's parables. Few mature Christians comprehend the trouble that lies ahead—before the rapture occurs. Thus, most believers are aloof and even out-of-touch concerning the signs of Christ's appearance and the rapture.

God in his faithfulness will remedy this "sleepy" condition and bring forth a final true move of God by his Spirit. He will use true servants of Christ who have awakened and have become ready to lead and teach by example.

This coming sovereign move of God's Holy Spirit is what we refer to as the midnight cry awakening as explained in the Parable of the Ten Maidens in Matthew 25:1-13. This coming event is also explained in the good news of the coming kingdom found in Matthew 24:14 and in the Parable of the Weeds recorded in Matthew 13:24-51.

An important aspect of our mission is to ensure each committed participant of MCCF becomes a fellowship team member ready to be used of God when the midnight cry is sounded as explained in the Parable of the Ten Maidens. When this final move of God begins, MCCF and other likeminded ministries and fellowships must be ready for a large influx of frightened and confused Christians as well as lost souls—where many will suffer and struggle with various emotional and mental problems.

---

[5] Matthew 7:21-23: *"Not everyone who says to me, 'Lord, Lord,' will enter the kingdom of heaven, but the one who does the will of my Father who is in heaven. On that day many will say to me, 'Lord, Lord, did we not prophesy in your name, and cast out demons in your name, and do many mighty works in your name?' And then will I declare to them, 'I never knew you; depart from me, you workers of lawlessness.'"*

Coming Away and Breaking the Spell
Dynamics of Spiritual and Emotional Abuse—Help for the Wounded Christian

False doctrine has allowed Satan to keep millions of born-again Christians in bondage to the power of their old carnal nature. Many spiritually and emotionally wounded people come to Christ, and then go to church where they receive instructions to ignore, cover up, or counterbalance instability through religious willpower, carnal spiritualism, or divide themselves by learning to create/develop a Christian personality.

Christian personality creation is a common trap for most believers, where inner issues, impurities, and ill carnal nature structures are masked by an outer personality that tries to mimic the Christian lifestyle. Despite all this hard work in suppressing their carnal nature—sooner than later, many who are taught to transform themselves into a Christian personality are overtaken by these deeply buried issues of heart. False teachings that help suppress past trauma and defilements are very popular.

Most symptoms experienced are from past-unresolved wounds and defilements and are swept under the rug or pretended away through use of false doctrine. Over the last five decades these false teachings have left many to languish without hope or forced to seek secular help.

We consider this type of instruction and care to be false and abusive to God's people. The prophet Jeremiah spoke on behalf of God, in his day, concerning this same type of cover up and mesmerization of God's people.

Jeremiah wrote, *"For from the least to the greatest of them, everyone is greedy for unjust gain; and from prophet to priest, everyone deals falsely. They have healed the wound of my people lightly, saying, 'Peace, peace,' when there is no peace. Were they ashamed when they committed abomination? No, they were not at all ashamed; they did not know how to blush. Therefore they shall fall among those who fall; at the time that I punish them, they shall be overthrown,' says the LORD"* (Jeremiah 6:13-15).

What is more disheartening, those wounded new Christians are further hurt and wounded by God's people who are ignorant, selfish, and hypocritical. Very little is addressed within Christian churches and fellowships concerning the self-righteousness and abusive arrogance that is now prominent, which has become very toxic.

Fellowships who embrace false teachings corrode true faith with hopelessness and bitterness concerning God's love, grace, and mercy. Masses of wounded believers are languishing within church and many are leaving Christian churches, feeling rejected and disenfranchised.

Some in leadership are beginning to address the enormous disconnect between the teaching of a watered-down Gospel of Christ and today's state of God's people. Anne Graham Lotz is one prominent Evangelical leader peeling back the pretense and veneer with one of her latest books, *Wounded by God's People.*[6]

When the Gospel of Christ is presented in the context of sound doctrine and the principles of Biblical sanctification—then healing and recovery for the wounded and emotionally damaged Christian is understood, embraced, and obtained.

MCCF presents sound doctrine and the Biblical principles to help the Holy Spirit facilitate healing and recovery for God's wounded. A vital aspect of recovery of a successful fellowship is providing prayer and support group meetings.

Our recovery principles and ministry came about through years of counseling wounded and troubled Christians, intense study of Scripture, and dependence on the work and gifts of the Holy Spirit. MCCF

---

[6] Anne Graham Lotz, *Wounded by God's People, Discovering How God's Love Heals our Hearts* (Grand Rapids, Mich.: Zondervan, 2013). Anne is the daughter of Billy Graham and is pioneering a much-needed exposé of the hypocrisy and abuse in church. For years evangelists and preachers on a national and international platform (like Anne's father Billy Graham) have led crusade upon crusade drawing masses of new converts to Christ and then shuffling them off to church—only to have millions become wounded by God's people running the local church, carelessly and selfishly. Masses of born-again believers have been driven from church, where many fall away from God, give up on God's people and quit going to fellowship altogether.

incorporates mentoring and recovery teamwork led by the Holy Spirit in bringing healing, transformation, and empowerment in Christ.

We follow the Apostle Paul's exhortation, *"Bear one another's burdens, and so fulfill the law of Christ"* (Galatians 6:2). With this intense prayer and burden bearing ministry we also mentor and support the sincere yet struggling Christian in learning how to work out their *"own salvation with fear and trembling, for it is God who works in you, both to will and to work for his good pleasure"* (Philippians 2:12-13). The most important aspect with individual recovery is exercising one's own faith and doing one's part in working with the Holy Spirit. Each must do the work, for faith without working out one's salvation is dead. (See James 2:14-25.)

We offer an introductory handbook for those interested in finding out more about God's principles in helping wounded and troubled Christians recover. This work is entitled: Crushed in Spirit 2nd Edition; *Help for Christians Suffering from a Wounded and Broken Spirit* and is available to order using ISBN 978-1-943412-16-7. Another publication is *Nomad Christians* ISBN 978-1-9434120-3-7, bringing incite and direction for the wounded and disenfranchised Christian wondering in life without safe and true fellowship.

At MCCF, you will find that we emphasize growing in maturity and stability for every believer, and teach how to avoid elitism, superficiality, and pretense or disingenuousness. God's people need to learn to embrace the Gospel of Christ by becoming Christlike in character. So that they, now being part of the body of Christ, truly become instruments of God in the healing of the wounded and confused convert. Further, we are determined to lead by example newcomers and new coverts to Christ who come to fellowship for care, and help break the spell of religiosity and churchianity. [7]

Choosing the Narrow Gate and the Hard Path

In his days on Earth, Jesus warned the crowds who followed him about the difficulties involved in knowing and obeying God. Christ said: *"Enter by the narrow gate. For the gate is wide and the way is easy that leads to destruction, and those who enter by it are many. For the gate is narrow and the way is hard that leads to life, and those who find it are few"* (Matthew 7:13-14).

Few Christians, when they first became believers weren't told and warned on what to expect in becoming a disciple of Christ. At first faith in Christ is exciting, however few understand that becoming born-again is just the beginning of a journey in growing up into salvation. Trials, testing, learning, and understanding one's own hidden issues of heart, along with Satan's opposition. It many ways life becomes hard.

New Christians tend to filter issues of heart and learn to mimic holiness and righteousness. Many are told that God wants to give the Christian the "abundant life" but are shocked when trouble comes and up pops an "old nature" way of feeling and reacting. The following passage from the books of James explains what God is doing by allowing trials and challenges to come our way.

"Blessed is the man who remains steadfast under trial, for when he has stood the test he will receive the crown of life, which God has promised to those who love him. Let no one say when he is tempted, "I am being tempted by God," for God cannot be tempted with evil, and he himself tempts no one. But each person is tempted when he is lured and enticed by his own desire. Then desire when it has conceived gives birth to sin, and sin when it is fully grown brings forth death" (James 1:12-15).

Sooner than later, following Christ will become challenging, but that is God's way of cleansing, healing purifying and transforming the inner being and heart so as to walk in the fulness of God's presence. It is important to understand what Jesus meant about following the hard way that leads to life or as James describes the end goal of God is that we receive the crown of life. Many confuse the meaning of the word "life" in these passages.

---

[7] Jesus confronted a same evil that became rooted in the Temple worship of his day, *"Woe to you, scribes and Pharisees, hypocrites! For you travel across sea and land to make a single proselyte [convert], and when he becomes a proselyte, you make him twice as much a child of hell as yourselves" (Matthew 23:15).* We refer to this as insincere faith, (not faith in Christ) but in being religious and playing church, "churchianity."

Overcoming the Abundant Life Syndrome

For most Christians, the abundant life in Christ has become misconstrued and confused with the American dream, good-times, and prosperity on earth—the "abundant life" on Earth is a doctrine inspired by hell that has many sincere believers struggling in a lukewarm faith, asleep during the darkest hour of the church age.

We must understand what Christ meant by the abundant life that he promises; if we do not, our powers of discernment will be skewed by carnal immaturity. The cares of this life will cause us to try to follow Christ, yet we will find ourselves stumbling in the dark with a few glimmering lights of hope here and there.

Jesus said of himself, *"I came that they may have* life *and have it abundantly"* (John 10:10). Again, Jesus taught, *"Enter by the narrow gate. For the gate is wide and the way is easy that leads to destruction, and those who enter by it are many. For the gate is narrow and the way is hard that leads to* life*, and those who find it are few"* (Matthew 7:13, 14).

What kind of life is Christ talking about in these two passages? The original Greek word for life in these two passages is Zōē, meaning the life we receive from Father God through Christ his son.

The other life that Jesus often spoke of is identified as *psuchē* in the original language that the Gospels were written in, where he states *"If anyone comes to me and does not hate his own father and mother and wife and children and brothers and sisters, yes, and even his own life, he cannot be my disciple. Whoever does not bear his own cross and come after me cannot be my disciple"* (Luke 14:26, 27).

Here in this passage, psuchē life denotes our natural life on earth or the seat of personality for our own life. This life is developed in the world, in family, and in significant relationships and grows into dynamic dependencies—all based upon humanity's fallen sin nature.

Before we come to Christ and spiritually meet our heavenly Father, we derive our self-worth and our sense of wellbeing from this relationship-driven psuchē life. All too often, the psuchē life becomes controlling, demanding, self-centered, even idolatrous, and often abusive. Thus, this natural life is the primary ingredient of the carnal life or life of the flesh that Scripture describes as being detrimental to the life of God within the believer's walk.

The Apostle Paul describes a battle between God's Spirit and our carnal psuchē life within us. As believers we are to enter this battle as a process of learning to overcome our carnal nature by killing not suppressing our old nature passions and desires. The Apostle states, *"But I say, walk by the Spirit, and you will not gratify the desires of the flesh. For the desires of the flesh are against the Spirit, and the desires of the Spirit are against the flesh, for these are opposed to each other, to keep you from doing the things you want to do"* (Galatians 5:16-17).

Zōē life in Christ (the potential abundant life we have with Father God in Christ) is often in opposition with our carnal or psuchē life (life we have grown accustomed to in the world, having worldly pleasures).

For the sincere Christian, the pleasures and demands of this world (relationships, occupation, hobbies, vacations, etc.) often oppose God's will. The things of this world and the love for them conflicts with God's presence within us and will often lead us away from God's work and his plans for us.

Review the following passage: *"Do not love the world or the things in the world. If anyone loves the world, the love of the Father is not in him. For all that is in the world—the desires of the flesh and the desires of the eyes and pride of life—is not from the Father but is from the world. And the world is passing away along with its desires, but whoever does the will of God abides forever"* (1 John 2:15-17).

Therefore, Christ commands that we hate the pleasures, demands, and the weights of the psuchē (soulish) aspect of our life, where we have developed a carnal worldly affection—within ourselves, and in its power within our relationships.

The carnal-psuchē life is not just our influence upon others but also its influence on us from others, including significant family members, extended family members, and our friends in the world. It is the carnal-psuchē life that most believers mistakenly want more of, which becomes easily confused with the life that Christ said he came to give, *"I came that they may have life and have it abundantly."*

The psuchē life dictates that we live for others and for our self, and often selfishly demand that others live for us—so that we humans, in our fallen sinful state become gods to each other and for each other.

The most harmful characteristics of this natural life are listed in Galatians: *"Now the works of the flesh are evident: sexual immorality, impurity, sensuality, idolatry, sorcery, enmity, strife, jealousy, fits of anger, rivalries, dissensions, divisions, envy, drunkenness, orgies, and things like these. I warn you, as I warned you before, that those who do such things will not inherit the kingdom of God"* (Galatians 5:19-21).

However, the characteristics of the Zōē life in Christ are as follows: *"The fruit of the Spirit is love, joy, peace, patience, kindness, goodness, faithfulness, gentleness, self-control; against such things there is no law"* (Galatians 5:22-23).

This life in God is obtained by entering a journey where the carnal-psuchē life dies and it is replaced by the Holy Spirit filled Zōē life, which is to become the believer's own life within.

Thus, the Apostle Paul finishes his explanation on the carnal-psuchē life by writing, *"And those who belong to Christ Jesus have crucified the flesh with its passions and desires"* (Galatians 5:24). Now review this harder teaching of Christ, *"For the gate is narrow and the way is hard that leads to <u>life</u>, and those who find it are few"* (Matthew 7:14).

The work of crucifying or dying to the carnal-psuchē life is not easy and often requires giving up or minimizing relationships that are based on the natural-worldly-carnal life.

At MCCF, we refer to Christians who embrace the prosperity message and yet struggle to achieve a successful materially blessed life, as suffering from the "abundant life syndrome."

Simply put, few Christians are taught the difference between the meaning of the abundant life in Christ and the carnal-worldly life of the world. A carnal-worldly life is how many find happiness by developing the sense of wellbeing and self-identity from relationships, work, ministry, lifestyle preferences, hobbies, sports, education, material possessions (i.e., the car one drives), money, and all other manner of activities.

Based on these explanations of the work of the cross within the believer's life, MCCF stresses that each member understands and embraces the Holy Spirit's work of opposing our fleshly desires. This leads to our daily dying to the carnal life so that the abundant life with the Father, through Christ, can be received.

Working with Troubled and Unstable Believers

Jesus responded to the Pharisees, who questioned his association with sinners and those of ill repute, by saying, *"Those who are well have no need of a physician, but those who are sick. Go and learn what this means, 'I desire mercy, and not sacrifice.' For I came not to call the righteous, but sinners"* (Matthew 9:12-13).

Many hurting sinners become believers and still struggle in their walk with Christ, continuing to lead unstable lives. Part of MCCF's mission is to provide ministry and resources for troubled believers. This means that those in ministry with us, who may not be as wounded as others, will need to learn to work with troubled believers and sinners who are coming for help and are genuinely seeking understanding and healing. They need mentoring and discipling help to learn how to work with the Lord to be transformed and grow to maturity and stability in Christ.

There may be times where you will need to minister and help another brother or sister overcome a pressing issue. Each member of the fellowship team is expected to learn how to minister effectively to wounded and troubled Christians at various levels, without becoming ensnared by game players and those who abuse the care giving aspects of a burden bearing ministry.

Fellowship team members learn how to support and guide a newcomer to the right ministry and provide complimentary support for growth in Christ and if necessary, help determine if a new believer is need of counseling and support group ministries.

Hidden, Unresolved Rage: Wounded Christians often suffer from past abuse (usually occurring during childhood) that form inner pools of rage, other damaged emotions, and wounds to their personal spirit. Through many years of counseling the resounding symptom buried deep within wounded Christians is "rage" directly connected to the belief that God allowed the abuse to occur and that God hates them.

The past abuse incited anger deep within the child's heart and psyche. This anger was left to foment over time and gave opportunity to Satan creating all manner wrong inner beliefs about self, others, God, and life. *"Fathers, do not provoke your children to anger, but bring them up in the discipline and instruction of the Lord"* (Ephesians 6:4).

Unfortunately, dysfunctional, and abusive family systems had parents, (especially fathers) who deliberately provoked their children to anger. Throughout childhood the provoked anger ferments into deep pools of rage that the demonic can incite years later.

"Be angry and do not sin; do not let the sun go down on your anger, and give no opportunity to the devil" (Ephesians 4:26-27). Troubled believers often find that their faith in their heavenly father is based on bad fathering during childhood, creating a deep-seated anger and even hatred towards God—yet undetected until denial is broken during recovery.

Confidentiality and Abuse

As a fellowship, it is important that gossip and meddling be avoided, where confidentiality of each fellow saint in attendance is maintained. Speaking out of turn about issues, difficulties, and the misfortunes of others causes rumors as well as malicious and base suspicions. However, sinful, abusive, and destructive behaviors are to be disclosed if observed by a person attending the fellowship. Destructive and abusive issues should be reported to leadership as soon as possible. (See 1 Corinthians 1:11 and 5:1.)

Fellowship mentors and leaders are to be confided with when troubling issues arise or when sins are confessed. Pastoral counseling is held in the highest confidentiality and what is shared in counseling; both the counselor and counselee confidentiality is to be kept in the highest security (top secret).

However, there may be sins, or threat of harm discovered in counseling that will require notification to the authorities;[8] As to any public disclosure about issues and struggles concerning anyone, there must be approval from all involved and subject to leadership's discretion and guidance.

We all make mistakes where we slipup and speak out of turn or meddle in the affairs of others, not trusting God for them. When mistakes are ignored, and correction is resisted, then individuals in fellowship are at risk of being maligned and abused through gossip, meddling, and busybody sinfulness. Abuse, in any form, within the fellowship family will not be tolerated and correction will be administered promptly and, in some cases, when a person persists in sinning, fellowship discipline will be exercised.[9]

Dealing with the Contrary

False brethren, who pretend to serve Christ but hold to a hidden agenda, can and often invade fellowships and congregations. This happens primarily because of the lack of discernment. Walking in discernment is a priority for all the believers attending MCCF.

The false often appear sincere, helpful, righteous, and they flatter others to gain advantage in relationships. Usually, this stems from bitter jealousy and selfish ambition. This type of insincere person professes to know Christ but opposes sound doctrine that holds those in fellowship accountable to genuine worship, pure motives, healthy fellowship, and a sincere faith and growth in Christ.

The apostle Paul instructed the following: *"I appeal to you, brothers, to watch out for those who cause divisions and create obstacles contrary to the doctrine that you have been taught; avoid them. For such persons do not serve our Lord Christ, but their own appetites, and by smooth talk and flattery they deceive the hearts of the naive. For your obedience is*

---

[8] Additional information is available for our burden bearing ministry upon request. This program employs Biblical principles and pastoral counseling in helping wounded Christians receive God's healing grace to overcome a wounded spirit and damaged emotions.

[9] Fellowship Discipline: MCCF leadership is responsible to maintain good conduct and Christlike moral standards within the fellowship. When a person resists correction and continues in harmful/sinful behavior that person can expect confrontation from the fellowship leaders or even another team member. *"As for those who persist in sin, rebuke them in the presence of all, so that the rest may stand in fear. In the presence of God and of Christ Jesus and of the elect angels I charge you to keep these rules without prejudging, doing nothing from partiality"* (1 Timothy 5:20-21). *"As for a person who stirs up division, after warning him once and then twice, have nothing more to do with him, knowing that such a person is warped and sinful; he is self-condemned"* (Titus 3:10-11).

known to all, so that I rejoice over you, but I want you to be wise as to what is good and innocent as to what is evil. The God of peace will soon crush Satan under your feet. The grace of our Lord Jesus Christ be with you" (Romans 16:17-20).

Avoid Them: Some people coming to fellowship prove to be self-centered and incorrigible and must be exposed and dealt with appropriately. Often the result is that those who are insubordinate and persist in undermining the health of the fellowship leave on their own accord when confronted, being unwilling to repent and change. Some however must be asked to leave.

Through many years of ministry and pastoral counsel, we have learned that the harder Scriptures, when applied properly, are effective in dealing with those people who prove to be incorrigible. For the sake of the sincere—as we desire to care properly for them—swift and direct confrontation must be exercised. We practice dis-fellowshipping with those who refuse to be corrected in order to spare any harm to others who are genuine, yet still vulnerable. Most of the time this confrontation will correct the carnal believer or drive out the evil imposter. Yes, many often prove to be evil in heart and live as being accursed troublemakers.[10]

In another passage the Apostle Paul warned of godlessness in the last days, where evil people will have the appearance of godliness, but denying its power. Paul exhorts us to "Avoid such people." The key is walking in true discernment and avoid trying to correct such a person or lead such a person to Christ. MCCF stresses that we minister and witness to those people whom God is working with and avoid those whom God has given over to a base mind. (See Romans 1:18-32.)

Wicked and Evil People

As the end-of-this-age unfolds, the number of evil and wicked people will grow exponentially [more and more rapidly]. The Apostle Paul requested prayer for himself and the ministry team in his letter to the Christians in Thessalonica: *"Finally, brothers, pray for us, that the word of the Lord may speed ahead and be honored, as happened among you, and that we may be delivered from wicked and evil men. For not all have faith"* (2 Thessalonians 3:1-2).

The fact that not all people have faith is sometimes hard to understand until you encounter someone who is evil within the core of their inner being. Often this type of man or woman gains entrance to fellowship by exhibiting an outer personality that seems to be religious and holy. The Apostle Paul tells us, *"I appeal to you, brothers, to watch out for those who cause divisions and create obstacles contrary to the doctrine that you have been taught; avoid them. For such persons do not serve our Lord Christ, but their own appetites, and by smooth talk and flattery they deceive the hearts of the naive. For your obedience is known to all, so that I rejoice over you, but I want you to be wise as to what is good and innocent as to what is evil. The God of peace will soon crush Satan under your feet. The grace of our Lord Jesus Christ be with you"* (Romans 16:17-20).

Christ warns that at the end of this age Satan will succeed in causing much trouble by injecting evil people throughout the world and into Christian churches. (See Parable of the Weeds Matthew 13:24-30; 36-43.)

The first step in discerning an evil person is accepting the fact that not all have faith, and that Satan knows how to groom and implant his evil human beings amongst family, friends, business, politics, and church.

For a deeper explanation about wicked and evil people, we recommend the following publication:
- **Will the Gates of Hell Prevail?** ISBN 978-1-943412

Maintaining Fellowship Integrity and Holiness

In the light of the growing perversions accepted and fostered by the culture we now live in, and its legality—it is vital that our fellowship's literature and legal documents are clear on our stance concerning the Biblical terms of immorality. Our moral position on homosexual, heterosexual perversion, and deliberate sinning and other immoral behaviors is clear.

---

[10] Peter wrote concerning those who profess to be Christian but do not embrace character changing sound doctrine, will live contrary to true Christlike behavior. Peter called certain types of false believers accursed children; *"But these, like irrational animals, creatures of instinct, born to be caught and destroyed, blaspheming about matters of which they are ignorant, will also be destroyed in their destruction, suffering wrong as the wage for their wrongdoing. They count it pleasure to revel in the daytime. They are blots and blemishes, reveling in their deceptions, while they feast with you. They have eyes full of adultery, insatiable for sin. They entice unsteady souls. They have hearts trained in greed. Accursed children!"* (2 Peter 2:12-14).

Gay marriage, homosexuality, and any other perverted lifestyles flaunted by individuals or groups are what MCCF considers deliberate sinning in the eyes of God and are clearly depicted and condemned in Scripture. It is our religious freedom and our moral obligation to maintain a no tolerance position in dealing with those attempting to force God's people to accept and even embrace their wicked lifestyle choices and sinfulness in fellowship or in certain endeavors.

To be clear, as based on Scripture, a God sanctioned marriage is to be only between man and woman, male and female not in any other manner. This Biblical doctrine makes it clear that gay marriage, marriage between male and male or female and female is not acceptable in the Scriptures and before the eyes of God. In fact, it is declared in Scripture as an abomination (an outrage and a disgrace).

However, unbelievers who choose to live in this kind of sin or any sinful lifestyle should not be condemned, warned, or confronted by a believer. It is MCCF's position to not attack, point the finger, demonstrate hatefulness, or attempt to convert any person involved in these kinds of sinful activities or any other sinful lifestyle.

Many involved in this type of rebellion and perversion have been given over to a debased mind by the hand of God. (See Romans 1:18-32.) Thus, confronting, correcting, evangelizing, or targeting people in such a condition will just bring abuse and does not lend to bringing their conscience around to help encourage repentance. *"Whoever corrects a scoffer gets himself abuse, and he who reproves a wicked man incurs injury. Do not reprove a scoffer, or he will hate you; reprove a wise man, and he will love you. Give instruction to a wise man, and he will be still wiser; teach a righteous man, and he will increase in learning"* (Proverbs 9:7-9).

Most that live in an extremely perverted and sinful lifestyle have seared their conscience and now scoff at God's decrees. The Apostle Paul wrote the following in the book of Romans to help us understand the reasons why it is futile to try to correct this kind of wickedness: *"And since they did not see fit to acknowledge God, God gave them up to a debased mind to do what ought not to be done. They were filled with all manner of unrighteousness, evil, covetousness, malice. They are full of envy, murder, strife, deceit, maliciousness. They are gossips, slanderers, haters of God, insolent, haughty, boastful, inventors of evil, disobedient to parents, foolish, faithless, heartless, ruthless. Though they know God's decree that those who practice such things deserve to die, they not only do them but give approval to those who practice them"* (Romans 1:28-32).

Jesus warned that in the last days this same type of culture would arise as it did in Sodom and Gomorrah. Lot and his family had to endure the depravity performed by wicked people of those two cities.[11] Finally, they were led away by angels of the Lord, just before destruction fell upon all the inhabitants of these cities. In the process of receiving the two angels (appearing as men), Lot had to confront a band of marauding homosexuals who wanted to sexually assault Lot's guests. Lot was threatened by the wicked as follows, *"They said, 'Stand back!' And they said, 'This fellow came to sojourn, and he has become the judge! Now we will deal worse with you than with them.' Then they pressed hard against the man Lot, and drew near to break the door down"* (Genesis 19:9).

The homosexual men of Sodom became enraged and threatened Lot, then tried to break down his door to invade his home and rape him and his guests. Now today we see a similar irrational and defiling attack on any ministry that confronts or attempts to correct people given over to this kind of wickedness. The LGBTQ+ (Lesbian, Gay, Bisexual, Transgender, Queer) lobby is becoming bold and abusive as they dole out attacks upon any opposition to their agenda; economically, politically, slanderously and in some cases physically.

Our approach to ministry for those stuck in this kind of bondage, (if they still have a conscience and faith) is to offer ministry if they opt-in (ask) to receive our support in counsel.

Adults desiring to renounce homosexuality as a believer in Christ must sign a disclaimer. In writing they must state that they are seeking our support, counsel, and fellowship by their own free will and

---

[11] *"He [God] rescued righteous Lot, greatly distressed by the sensual conduct of the wicked (for as that righteous man lived among them day after day, he was tormenting in his righteous soul over their lawless deeds that he saw and heard)"* (2 Peter 2:7-8).

volition—that they have not been compelled or pressured by MCCF or any of its staff or members to renounce homosexuality or any sinful lifestyle.

Any believer attending MCCF who regresses, falls back into, or chooses to belligerently practice or maintains any sinful lifestyle or sinful alliance (openly or secretly) and does not repent will be asked to leave the fellowship.

The following passage lays a foundation for avoiding those who call themselves Christian yet maintain a sinful lifestyle purposely. *"I wrote to you in my letter not to associate with sexually immoral people—not at all meaning the sexually immoral of this world, or the greedy and swindlers, or idolaters, since then you would need to go out of the world. But now I am writing to you not to associate with anyone who bears the name of brother if he is guilty of sexual immorality or greed, or is an idolater, reviler, drunkard, or swindler—not even to eat with such a one. For what have I to do with judging outsiders? Is it not those inside the church whom you are to judge? God judges those outside. 'Purge the evil person from among you'"* (1 Corinthians 5:9-13).

The Gift, Gifts, and the Baptism of the Holy Spirit

The work and power of the Holy Spirit is one of the most controversial subjects debated and researched over the last fifty years. With the Wales Revival[12] starting at the turn of the twentieth century, along with other movements, the gift of the Holy Spirit and the gifts of the Holy Spirit have emerged as a major work of God in restoring divine power to the body of Christ.

We believe every believer must receive the gift of the Holy Spirit. This experience is marked by peace and a sense of closeness to God. However, this experience is often confused with the baptism of the Holy Spirit for power and ministry.

The Apostles received the Holy Spirit long before they were baptized by the Holy Spirit to be empower for ministry on the day of Pentecost. (See John 20:19-22.)

There may be other manifestations when receiving the Holy Spirit. These "other manifestations" should not be exalted, but rather tested and monitored for authenticity. Lack of testing and poor discernment has allowed demonic counterfeiting of the gifts to become popular and widespread, producing extreme and wild manifestations, confusion, and divisions within the body of Christ.[13]

The fruit of the Holy Spirit as explained in Galatians 5:22-26 should be the indicator or sign sought among believers to verify that a believer has received the gift of the Holy Spirit with the desire to be continually filled with the Holy Spirit and to walk (live) in holiness.

The gift of the Holy Spirit is given to each sincere and genuine believer in Christ who asks to be filled with the Holy Spirit, provided they are not secretly sinning. Simon the magician in the book of Acts wanted to have the power of the Holy Spirit in his life for the wrong reasons, so desirous that he offered money to buy the power of God.

The Apostle Peter identified this new believer's error by stating, *"For I see that you are in the gall of bitterness and in the bond of iniquity"* (Acts 8:23). Many believers seek the infilling of the Holy Spirit in error and never receive correction, which leads many to receive a counterfeiting demon in the place of the Holy Spirit.

The Holy Spirit's presence within each believer has many benefits, both for ministry and in life and is essential in advancing the Gospel of Christ. The Holy Spirit is the personal manifestation of God and works

---

[12] The Welsh Revival (1904–1905) was the largest Christian revival in Wales during the 20th century. The Welsh (Wales) revival also was one of the most dramatic in terms of its effect on the population, and it had repercussions that reached far beyond the Welsh border, triggering a series of revivals in other countries. The Wales revival is considered the move of God in modern church history that restored the gifts of the Holy Spirit back to the body of Christ.

[13] We use the term "body of Christ" as do most Protestants denominations and non-denominations to collectively describe believers in Christ, as opposed to only those who are members of the Catholic Church. In this sense, Christians are members of the universal body of Christ not because of identification with the institution of a physical church, but through identification with Christ directly through faith. (See Romans 12:5, 1 Corinthians 12:12-27, Ephesians 3:6 and 5:23, Colossians 1:18 and Colossians 1:24.) In using the term, the "body of Christ," Jesus Christ is seen as the "head" of the body, the body being the church, while the "members" of the body are seen as members of the Church.

in many ways in the life of the believer for growth, maturity, discernment and understanding the truth of Scripture. The Holy Spirit's presence in the believer's life should not be confused with the gifts of the Holy Spirit. Those who desire the gifts of the Holy Spirit for ministry should be led by the Holy Spirit, supported, mentored, and corrected by mature fellow Christians and leadership.

The gifts should not be sought and practiced for self-glorification. Therefore, the motives and the intentions of the heart should be exposed through the discipline of the Lord and the work of the cross—before seeking any gift of the Holy Spirit. Many have wrong motives in seeking the gifts of the Holy Spirit and do not become mature in Christ, in his discipline and training; again, this is a dangerous condition and is a problem experienced throughout the body of Christ where counterfeit gifts from the devil and his minions become manifest.

The passions and desires of the flesh produce the works of the flesh as explained in Galatians 5:16-21. Those deceitful, selfish, and sinful desires are to be put to death, so that the person of the Holy Spirit may not be grieved or forced to abandon a believer. Many Christians grieve and offend the presence of the Holy Spirit because of deliberate sinning, disobedience, or ministering out of wrong reasons.

Many receive false or counterfeit gifts because they lust after the power of God and live in an unrepentant state of heart, lacking humility while ministering and living in their own carnal energies.

Again, as stated, the work of the cross is a process that should be embraced until the believer is sanctified sufficiently and walks in the gifts humbly and graciously. Leadership should challenge power-seeking Christians and correct out-of-control Christians who lust for the gifts of the Holy Spirit, even if it means driving out the unrepentant carnal Christian from fellowship.

Often, we found ourselves dealing with wolves in sheep's clothing; these Christian imposters learn to walk in a counterfeit faith manifesting or practicing counterfeit spiritual gifts where their character will eventually bear witness to their evil motives.

The book of Jude describes specifically this type of marauding false believer, *"These are grumblers, malcontents, following their own sinful desires; they are loud-mouthed boasters, showing favoritism to gain advantage. But you must remember, beloved, the predictions of the apostles of our Lord Jesus Christ. They said to you, 'In the last time there will be scoffers, following their own ungodly passions. It is these who cause divisions, worldly people, devoid of the Spirit'"* (Jude 16-19).

Unfortunately, these false believers are everywhere and deceive many. This last day's condition of the false invading the body of Christ plagues many fellowships and calls for keen discernment. Therefore, leadership at MCCF and the saints in attendance learn to practice discernment and are willing to exercise discipline and confront the wayward.

The gift that all mature Christians should seek after is the gift of prophecy, in the love of God. This cuts to the chase and leaves no room for the false. Much of prophecy practiced today only soothes and tickles the ear. Though prophecy should edify, it should not pacify sin, carnality, or condone hypocrisy—rather, it should operate to disclose the secrets of the heart, ill motives of heart, and secret sin. (See 1 Corinthians 14:24-25 and also later in this handbook.)

Indeed, there is much confusion concerning the gift of the Holy Spirit, the demonstrated power of God through the gifts, and the baptism of the Holy Spirit.

The gifts of the Holy Spirit will manifest as God wills and will work the appropriate gift or gifts into a believer's walk and ministry as needed, in conjunction with proper training and discipline. Do not lust after the power of God; rather seek the gifts as the Holy Spirit leads and make sure you are well on your way in having the character of Christ formed within you by embracing the discipline of the Lord. When we embrace all that Christ taught, a true servant will seek on a continual basis, the infilling of the Holy Spirit and maintain an intimate relationship with the living God.

Now is the time to learn discernment concerning false gifts and the spiritual power of the human spirit driven by the flesh. Human spirit power is frequently boosted by a counterfeiting demonic spirit.

This is where we must agree with sound doctrine in Scripture. We can guarantee that you will suffer disruptions, problems, and even demonic attacks if you vacillate on this issue. *"So, my brothers, earnestly desire to prophesy, and do not forbid speaking in tongues. But all things should be done decently and in order"* (1 Corinthians 14:39, 40).

False gifting will assert itself in fellowship and attempt to take control in the name of freedom of expression of the gifts of the Holy Spirit. The Apostle Paul had to set the church at Corinth straight on this matter by warning them that outsiders would think that they were mad in their uncontrolled exercise of spiritual expressions. (See 1 Corinthians 14:23-25.)

Movements that push for methods and experiences are what Christ warned about at the end-of-the-age. False doctrines devised by false teachers learn to proclaim another Jesus, a different spirit, and a different gospel than that which is found in the word of God. (See Matthew. 24:1-28 and 2 Corinthians 11:1-15).

Madness has invaded many Charismatic, Pentecostal, and Evangelical fellowships, exasperated by movements that continue to introduce more exotic experiences. Few have learned to discern the difference between counterfeit manifestations by the spiritual power of the demonic and the genuine work of the Holy Spirit. As mentioned earlier in this handbook, we recommend the following:

- "The Gift, Gifts, and Fruit of the Holy Spirit" ISBN 978-1-943412-45-7

The Gift of Prophesy
By Individuals and During Meetings

In 1 Corinthians chapter 14, the Apostle Paul plainly explains the importance of seeking the gifts of the Holy Spirit, and especially the gift of prophesy. *"Pursue love, and earnestly desire the spiritual gifts, especially that you may prophesy"* (1 Corinthians 14:1). In this chapter, the Apostle outlines the proper practice for individuals and for fellowship as a whole on how to deliver a prophesy or speak forth in a tongue.

Individually, we must submit to the discipline of the Lord in seeking the gift of prophesy or a language not of our own. The need to appear to others as spiritual or to draw attention to oneself must become crucified within our hearts and inner being. This means allowing the Holy Spirit to show wrong motives or mixed motives that are hidden within.

When we disassociate from our hidden wrong motives and pursue the gift of prophesy or a tongue, what we receive from the Holy Spirit will be skewed and interpreted inaccurately. Many Christians are taught that one must speak in a tongue as a sign of being baptized in the Holy Spirit.

However, the Apostles explains: *"Thus tongues are a sign not for believers but for unbelievers, while prophecy is a sign not for unbelievers but for believers. If, therefore, the whole church comes together and all speak in tongues, and outsiders or unbelievers enter, will they not say that you are out of your minds?"* (1 Corinthians 14:22-23).

The true gift of prophesy exposes secret issues the heart as explained by the Apostle Paul and if the gift of prophesy is real the secrets of the heart will be exposed. This gift is often used in counseling another who is suffering from past forgotten trauma or defilements: *"But if all prophesy, and an unbeliever or outsider enters, he is convicted by all, he is called to account by all, the secrets of his heart are disclosed, and so, falling on his face, he will worship God and declare that God is really among you"* (1 Corinthians 14:24-25).

At MCCF, those wanting to practice the gifts publicly during designated times and designated meetings are required to confirm with leadership to receive approval. Many Charismatic and Pentecostal Christians practice a counterfeit tongue and or proclaim soothing or condemning false prophesy. This is not allowed at MCCF.

Worship with Order and Decency

As mentioned, the Apostle Paul exhorted Christians in Corinth that *"all things should be done decently and in order"* (1 Corinthians 14:40). Our concern with worship is not giving place to carnal spiritualism in the guise of praise and worship. We have witnessed many fellowships fall under the spell of false praise and worship where the human spirit is stirred by music sung and played in a manner that exhibits worldliness and, in many cases, paganistic spiritualism.

Worship for many has evolved into a feeling-based experience, where the worshipper becomes enthralled with the desire to feel blissful emotions, produced by euphoric spiritualistic aura and sensuality. The act of worship becomes the focus of worship—where sincere worship and the desire to please God becomes almost entirely negated and relegated to a form of hypocrisy (acting).

Music is a powerful way of touching our emotions and our spirit—in many cases, in a manipulative manner. Movie soundtracks can use background music to prepare the audience for a scene that will be dramatic, violent, humorous, etc. Movies, music videos, and the many genres within the music industry cater to the various entertainment preferences of our culture.

Now, music has become a way of entertaining worshippers within many congregations where chorus selections are geared to stir and guide the congregation into a common mood. Worship music in congregations that are churchianity[14] orientated digress into an emotional or soulish[15] genre. The music played, and the chorus sung are designed and performed to change the mood of the congregants, rather than to come before God and worship him. This soulish type of worship is a subtle shift of focus, where the soul is aroused to delve inwardly to influence and awaken the personal spirit of the worshipper.

This is an angel of light work just as the Apostle Paul described as taking place within the church in Corinth (a very charismatic New Testament church). In this worked-up soulish state, the human spirit becomes aroused by this type of carnal activity, making an avenue for a demonic counterfeit spirit to seep in and boost the pleasurable aspects of activating and massaging one's own personal spirit.

Participants are led to believe they are entering the presence of the Holy Spirit by engaging in this form of soulish worship. Unfortunately, the spirit they enter is not the Holy Spirit but their own personal spirit unified with each other into a *strange harmonious synergy* of human spirits. The scary aspect is that worshippers are collectively manipulated to channel or conjure a demonic counterfeiting force.

Millions of deceived believers fall under the spell of the worship team's mesmerizing showmanship, and with the use of spiritualism and conjuring techniques much like the superstitious practices in pagan cultures.

This type of carnal praise and worship is shunned at MC Chapel Fellowship. However, we do encourage healthy and genuine praise and worship in song that is directed unto the Lord in holy reverence and awe, and humble sincerity of heart. When there is sincere and genuine worship, one may become broken and weep, confessing and repenting, while another may feel the Holy Spirit joy and peace and express exuberant joy.

We encourage the practice of the gifts of the Holy Spirit with song and worship. However, we inform and teach those in our care how to discern the obvious counterfeit as well as the subtler counterfeit praise and worship that are often manifested with false gifts.

Each believer must learn to enter the deeper presence of God with a genuine heart felt love toward God expressed in song and praise and be filled with the Holy Spirit expressing genuine manifestations of the Holy Spirit.

This genuine worship can only be experienced within the heart and spirit of believers who are maturing in Christ-like character, for those who have presented their life and body entirely as living sacrifices unto the Lord. The following passage helps explain this goal in achieving a pure and sincere life of worship and praise in Christ-like character: *"I appeal to you therefore, brothers, by the mercies of God, to present your bodies as a living sacrifice, holy and acceptable to God, which is your spiritual worship. Do not be conformed to this world, but be transformed by the renewal of your mind, that by testing you may discern what is the will of God, what is good and acceptable and perfect"* (Romans 12:1-2).

---

14 The term churchianity, in this context encompasses the emerging church movement, the purpose-driven church movement, and other mega-church, fast growth fellowships, as well as denominations and independent fellowships that pursue converts to their church organization instead of bringing them to Christ with the intent to grow each convert into a solid servant of Christ.

15 Soulish is another term that describes a carnal Christian. Soulish Christians function spiritually in the soul realm, where emotions and selfish motives drive their worship, ministry, and good works. In this context of worship, music stirs the emotions, or the soul and in-turn stirs the person's personal spirit. Mixing the soul and spirit to enter into a supposed "blessing," is usually void of the Holy Spirit.

MC Chapel Fellowship meetings that are purposed for fellowship worship, instruction, (primarily Sunday services) are to free of exotic-carnal spiritual expressions that are out of turn. Ministering a word of knowledge, prophesy, or exhortation are to be exercised by those members vetted and released to minister as such. Outsiders, newcomers, or visitors, or attendees not yet members are to refrain from expression of any giftings until they become a member of the fellowship or unless they are approved guests.

New attendees, visitors, or an outsider considering becoming a member or one who desires to attend on a regular basis—and would like to express themselves in any ministerial gifting or expression of a gift of the Holy Spirit, are required to present themselves to an Elder, a Staff Pastor, an Associate Pastor, or the Senior Pastor to be recognized and examined by the Board of Elders before any public display of any gifting or expression of a spiritual gift.

Indiscriminate speaking in an unknown tongue is not practiced in any MC Chapel Fellowship meetings. However, the gift of prophesy is allowed as a member once that member is qualified and released.

This may seem harsh, but considering the unbridled carnal spiritualism invading most fellowships, where false spiritual expressions pop up in maddening manifestations often result in hijacking meetings—this rule helps manage carnal spiritualism that squelches the genuine expression of the gifts of the Holy Spirit through disciplined servants of Christ.

True Leadership in the Body of Christ

Jesus warned that there would come false leaders to plague his Church, especially in the last days of this age: "And Jesus answered them, *"See that no one leads you astray. For many will come in my name, saying, 'I am the Christ,' and they will lead many astray"* (Matthew 24:4-5). In this passage, Christ means that false leaders will come in his name proclaiming that they know me, and present exclusive teachings on how to become Christlike, but their teachings focus on their version of Christ, leading many away from knowing and obeying the actual person of Christ. In the end many will following a false version of Christ by way of following the false leader who has put themselves as intermediators between their followers and God.

Also, Christ explained that in the last days false prophets would arise to mislead many: *"And many false prophets will arise and lead many astray"* (Matthew 24:11). There has arisen many false prophets who prophesy only good things and try to gain credibly to build up their own name and expand their brand (ministry). Further, networks of false prophets and false leaders who declare themselves to be Apostles mislead many through false prophesies and false teachings.

The following passage written by the Apostle Paul points out how Jesus does call leaders, trains and sends them to minister to God's people as gifts: *"But grace was given to each one of us according to the measure of Christ's gift. Therefore it says, "When he ascended on high he led a host of captives, and he gave gifts to men... And he gave the apostles, the prophets, the evangelists, the shepherds and teachers, to equip the saints for the work of ministry, for building up the body of Christ, until we all attain to the unity of the faith and of the knowledge of the Son of God, to mature manhood, to the measure of the stature of the fullness of Christ, so that we may no longer be children, tossed to and fro by the waves and carried about by every wind of doctrine, by human cunning, by craftiness in deceitful schemes.* (Ephesians 4:7-14).

Christ does call and take captive some to be recognized as true leaders filling the role of an apostles, prophets, evangelist, pastors, and teachers. These leaders are taken through severe discipline of the Lord and training so as to not cause people to follow themselves, but rather teach and minister God's people to become mature in Christ, following Christ exclusively.

In these last days carnal and false leaders will declare themselves to be an apostle, or prophet without being called by Christ and taken into the wilderness to become a genuine disciple and servant Christ. These wayward leaders persuade God's people to follow them and not become mature in the true Christ.

These false leaders brand themselves as apostles or prophet, declaring themselves to have authority that should be highly recognized. They love the title of apostle, prophet, evangelist, pastor, or teacher which gives them inner pride and sense of specialness so that others should receive instruction from them or be touched by their special anointing.

Those who prance and present their title as special were not called of Christ, let alone taken captive and disciplined in sever trials so that they dare not steal glory from Christ. They avoid the suffering of Christ and take the easy path that leads to destruction.

The Apostle Paul challenged those he termed "super apostles" who declared themselves special. Here is what Paul wrote about such deceitful men who called themselves apostles: *"And what I am doing I will continue to do, in order to undermine the claim of those who would like to claim that in their boasted mission they work on the same terms as we do. For such men are false apostles, deceitful workmen, disguising themselves as apostles of Christ. And no wonder, for even Satan disguises himself as an angel of light. So it is no surprise if his servants, also, disguise themselves as servants of righteousness. Their end will correspond to their deeds"* (2 Corinthians 11:12-15).

Meetings and their Purpose

Every meeting has a purpose that is meant to facilitate growth in Christ. There is a time for worship and praise, there is a time for instruction, exhortation, and prophesy, there is a time for confession and public prayer, there is a time for laying on of hands, there is a time solemn assembly and intercession, there is a time for individual mentoring and ministry, there is a time for heart felt contrition and brokenness, there is a time to experience the extra joy in the Lord that revies.

However, maturity in Christ and the discipline of the Lord produces the fruit of the Holy Spirit's presence dwelling in Christlike character. And that type of maturity and character transformation is the foundation for the peace and joy of God's abiding presence that is everlasting. This is accomplished by embracing the work of the cross within the believer life. [16]

One of the most discouraging issues for God's people today is the gross lack of the knowledge of God. Few rightly understand Scripture through faithful study and a willingness to learn and embrace all the written Word of God. A true disciples of Christ will hunger and willingly study the written word of God, allowing Scripture to become active and dynamically expose true motives and intentions of our heart and to develop a working relationship with the Living Word.

The "Living Word" is the written word of God made alive by the Holy Spirit that every sincere disciple of Christ must embrace. Through the study of God's word and discipline of the Lord comes the discerning of our own thoughts and intentions of the heart. God desires his people to know him personally, not know of him vicariously through teachers who mince and hash the word of God to validate their own agenda and schemes.

Unfortunately, most Christians engage in a self-driven approach to knowing God vicariously and eagerly embrace every wind of doctrine by smooth talking leaders. Thus, most believers never enter God's rest—where the Holy Spirit works through us, leading us away from working for God religiously. (Study Colossians 4:1-3, and Hebrews 4:11-13.)

Meetings at MC Chapel Fellowship are structured to encourage, strengthen, and challenge each fellowship team member to study God's word for themselves. MCCF leadership instruct and train fellowship members to refrain from allowing meetings to be taken over by participants or outsiders who promote wayward teachings that seem to be spiritual, but in the end derail growth in Christ and the study of God's word.

---

[16] Crucifying the works of the flesh: Many Christians are taught to take shortcuts in overcoming the emotional and spiritual internal angsts that all believers encounter when it comes to winning the war against the old carnal nature and its works. Carnal worship and spiritualism often help suppress the unwanted feelings that surface during this internal war on crucifying (brining to death) the root canal character structures of the old nature. Hidden past defilements, wounds, and unbelief often drive the desires and passions of the flesh. These root issues must be worked out and dealt with—not suppressed through ecstatic feelings that carnal spiritualism generates. *"And those who belong to Christ Jesus have crucified the flesh with its passions and desires"* (Galatians 5:24).

Leadership's goal is to make disciples that God can use in a mighty way, where Christ becomes head, and the Holy Spirit leads and guides each person with minimal carnal hindrance. Leaders are to help equip Christians to become disciples of Christ by observing all that Christ taught.

Unfortunately, many in leadership today manipulate followers to follow a leader, a doctrine, or a movement. The Apostle Paul warned Christians elders: *"I know that after my departure fierce wolves will come in among you, not sparing the flock; and from among your own selves will arise men speaking twisted things, to draw away the disciples after them"* (Acts 20:29-30).

Study Ephesians 4:11-16 carefully, it will help you understand our approach to meetings and leadership. There is no carnal formula or a spiritual manifestation that magically downloads the knowledge of God's word or miraculously creates Christ-like character. Growing up into salvation is simply hard work that requires a faith that holds to patience, trust, and obedience. Each must learn as the Apostle Paul put it: *"As you have <u>always obeyed</u>, so now, not only as in my presence but much more in my absence, <u>work out your own salvation with fear and trembling, for it is God who works in you, both to will and to work for his good pleasure</u>"* (Philippians 2:12-13).

Consensus and Accommodating Theology and Churchianity

The Apostle Paul forewarned that there would come a time when *"people will not endure sound teaching, but having itching ears they will accumulate for themselves teachers to suit their own passions, and will turn away from listening to the truth and wander off into myths"* (2 Timothy 4:3-5).

This prediction truly fits our time as we see many Christians clamor for teachers who preach and teach feel-good doctrines. Feel-good doctrines are teachings that accommodate carnal believers who want to sooth or negate bad feelings[17], and cater to selfishness, passions of the flesh and a worldly lifestyle.

Myths about God, Christ, and life that makes the walk with God seem easy undermine sound teachings found in Scripture. These mythical teachings contradict truth found in Scripture and the most popular myths become what we call consensus theology, where most theologians, preachers and teachers concede that these false teachings and myths are true because they are so popular.

Many pastors and teachers give themselves over to these popular, yet errant teachings where a consensus or an agreement is formed with each other. It is a form of cowing down by preaching and teaching what the people want to hear, not confronting and exhorting with sound teachings from the Scriptures that addresses what God's people need to hear.

Few in ministry challenge the popular teachings that suit the masses for fear of rejection or disapproval, as they compete for recognition and approval from the people. Most in leadership today fall into popularity contests with each other. This approach has seeped into church, fellowship, and congregations everywhere. People attend fellowship based on the popularity of the leader, the fellowship amenities, and the social and networking benefits, rather than to seek the lordship of Christ.

We refer to this religious experience by using the term "churchianity." Churchianity[18] is like what the Jews fell into with temple worship. Instead of gathering together to worship God and learn about God, they fell into the social activities and rituals of temple worship. They digressed from worshipping God in genuine sincerity. They fell prey to a system of worship and religious activities that took the place of knowing God and drawing closer to him.

---

[17] Bad feelings along with other emotional or mental issues are common symptoms or indicators of unresolved wounds to one's personal spirit along with damaged emotions. Demons often use these defilement and wounds of one's heart and spirit to plague and oppress, making life for the wounded-carnal believer a veritable hell. Thus, false doctrine and mythical teachings become attractive forms of anti-depressants and are embraced to help create sensuous feelings and false spirit manifestations that generate an inner euphoria to suppress bad feelings.

[18] We call the dynamic of "churchianity" to be defined as a disapproving condition where social and relationship practices in Christian religion have a larger emphasis placed upon church attendance than upon a solid relationship with God, where sound doctrine and deeper spiritual teachings of Scripture are no longer the focus. This religious dynamic forms habits of church life or the institutional traditions of the church to take precedence over having a right and true relationship with God. Churchianity is a condition of being too church-focused and less Christ centered.

Our attitude at MCCF is that Christ comes to bless and dwell with his people, when two or three are gathered in his name, not because of masses of people, a special facility, ornate building, carnal spiritualism, or a so-called anointed leader that mesmerizes through entertaining rhetoric and preaches a watered down Gospel.

Evangelism—Working Where God is Working

Church growth is big business today, bringing increased pressure upon pastors and elders to expand facilities and add amenities to attract new converts to Christ. Many have learned to entice the lost or the backslidden believer for all the wrong reasons, which encourages people not called of God, or born again to come to fellowship. This approach can also pressure others to become religious because they were told about the Gospel out of God's timing.[19]

As a fellowship, there are two basic principles we embrace in sharing the Gospel with the lost or those seeking a new church home:

1. We equip and build up those attending fellowship to become mature in Christ and able to mentor new converts before they are encouraged to evangelize others.
2. Those ready to share their testimony and their life in Christ with others must learn to work where God is working and not force others to come to Christ in the power of flesh (self-strength).

There are other Biblical principles that must be learned and mastered before launching any formal evangelistic outreach. The most important discipline every saint attending MCCF is discernment.

The Apostle Paul wrote, *"I appeal to you, brothers, to watch out for those who cause divisions and create obstacles contrary to the doctrine that you have been taught; avoid them. For such persons do not serve our Lord Christ, but their own appetites, and by smooth talk and flattery they deceive the hearts of the naive. For your obedience is known to all, so that I rejoice over you, but I want you to be wise as to what is good and innocent as to what is evil. The God of peace will soon crush Satan under your feet"* (Romans 16:17-20).

This is also our appeal, that those involved and committed to advancing the MCCF mission become wise concerning those who have a good heart and learn not be naïve and deceived by the many game players, false converts, and imposters coming to church—forcing upon the fellowship their own agenda. It is important that those added to our fellowship are called of God, born of the Spirit, and understand the cost of becoming a disciple of Christ. It is not easy following Christ and becoming his disciple, and will become more challenging as the last days persecution increases. [20]

Fellowship Government and Leadership, Bylaws, and Enrollment

Message of the Cross Chapel Fellowship (MCCF) is the fellowship ministry of Message of the Cross Global Ministries (MCGM).

The MCCF church government and leadership is set up and governed by the founding elders (directors) of Message of the Cross Global Ministries, by their agreement set forth in MCGM's bylaws. MCCF government is the board of founding elders of MCGM and consists of six (6) founding partners who have formed this non-denominational ministry and fellowship.

Many independent, non-denominational, and denominational fellowships have been seduced and succumb to various church growth methodologies and frameworks such as the Purpose Driven movement, which in some cases have led to hostile and destructive takeovers. To ensure stability and integrity, MCGM's and its Chapel Fellowship bylaws prevent this kind of divisive and destructive activity.

---

[19] Becoming religious is a major aspect of false church growth, where people become acquainted with the Gospel of Christ not having a true spiritual encounter with the living God. Most who become religious Christians become hardened towards receiving the true Christ as savior. They are born of the flesh religiously, not born of the Spirit of God. (See John 1:12-13 and Galatians 4:29.)

[20] Jesus warned: *"Whoever does not bear his own cross and come after me cannot be my disciple. For which of you, desiring to build a tower, does not first sit down and count the cost, whether he has enough to complete it? … So therefore, any one of you who does not renounce all that he has cannot be my disciple"* (Luke 14:27-28, 33). Christ demands that we relinquish any idolatrous ownership and control over all we possess in life—especially in relationships. Christian idolatry within relationship is a major problem throughout Christianity.

Fellowship Bylaws Overview

A copy of the MCGM/MCCF bylaws is given to each new MC Chapel Fellowship team member. In short, the bylaws are established to guide and direct the successful operation, administration, finances, fellowship discipline, ministries, and fellowship.

This fellowship handbook addresses the reasoning for much of the content of the ministry bylaws; however, each person attending must become familiar with the ministry bylaws as part of the enrollment process.

The following portions of this handbook, (statement of faith, fellowship commitment and fellowship agreement) convey the importance of adhering to sound doctrine from Scripture to guide the conduct, discipline, training and ministries of MC Global Ministries and its Chapel Fellowship.

Enrollment Process

Becoming a MC Chapel Fellowship team member is a commitment we take seriously. As a fellowship, enrollment is offered with open arms and open hearts to those who demonstrate fruit of Christ working within them.

Specifically, we enroll those called of God to be part of this fellowship and its work, with an additional prerequisite of a *demonstrated likeminded stance* with MCCF's statement of faith, bylaws, leadership, as well as our fellowship government and discipline guidelines.

Individuals who meet our fellowship team membership requirements will be publicly accepted in good standing as an active team member and shall receive the privileges and responsibilities of membership.

Steps to enrollment—Eligibility:

1. Beginning the enrollment process starts with consistent fellowship attendance for not less than a period of two months. (See Hebrews 10:23-25.)
2. Demonstrate evidence of a new birth experience and a consistent Christian life with a desire to bear fruit of repentance and emanate the fruit of the Spirit with a consistent desire to crucify the works of the flesh. (See John 1:12-13, 3:3-7; Acts 4:12; Romans 6:4, 10:9-10; Galatians 5:16-26; Ephesians 4:17-32, 5:1-2; 1 John 1:6, 7.)
3. Demonstrate a cooperative, accountable, teachable, and Christ-like spirit as instructed in Scripture. (See Ephesians 2:1-16.)
4. Commit to faithfully attend and participate in the meetings and ministries of the fellowship and contribute regularly in a cheerful manner without reluctance or compulsively, rather support the financial needs of the fellowship as determined prayerfully and in wisdom. (See 1 Corinthians 16:2; 2 Corinthians 9:7.)
5. Be 12 years of age, with voting privileges beginning at age 18. (Twelve years of age is considered the Biblical age of accountability and an appropriate age for water baptism.)
6. Subscribe to the statement of faith of the fellowship, the fellowship commitment, agree to, and sign the fellowship agreement.
7. Abstain from all immorality condemned in Scripture and falling into sinful alliances, secret sin, or sinning deliberately. Immorality and habitual-deliberate sinning shall be considered grounds for refusing membership or ejection from the roles of fellowship and exclusion from fellowship meetings.

Steps to enrollment—Process of Acceptance:

Definition: Membership in MCGM's Chapel Fellowship is a covenant partnership with individuals who have accepted and professed their faith in Jesus Christ as Savior and Lord. Members shall be in accord with the purpose, mission, statement of faith, bylaws, and the pastors and leaders of MC Chapel Fellowship. Individuals who have met membership requirements, who have been publicly accepted, and are in good standing as active attendee shall receive the privileges and responsibilities of membership.

MC Chapel Fellowship Membership Requirements: Any individual desiring membership in MCGM's Chapel Fellowship must pass the following requirements:

A. Demonstrate evidence of a new birth experience and a consistent, stable Christian life. (John 1:12-13, 3:3-7; Acts 4:12; Romans 6:4, 10:9-10; Ephesians 4:17-32, 5:1-2; 1 John 1:6, 7.)

B. Attend and Pass "What We Believe and Why" Fellowship Membership Class

C. A single man or single woman who has demonstrated loyalty to their pledge to serve Christ and refrains from lusting for a partner. (1 Timothy 5:11-14.)

D. Abstain from all immorality condemned in Scripture, including a lifestyle that is sexually immoral, such as LGBTQQ (lesbian, gay, bisexual, transgender, questioning, queer) or a drunkard, swindler, or troublemaker. (1 Corinthians 5:11-13.)

E. One who does not stir up division, strife, gossips, or meddles, and embraces correction. (1 Corinthians 5:9-13; Titus 3:10-11.) Those who do such and reject correction will be subject to disciplinary action and possibly barred from fellowship.

F. Fellowship ministry team member candidates are required to sign a confidentiality and disclosure agreement and submit to a criminal background check.

G. Fellowship members are required to hold the MC Chapel Fellowship Handbook and MC Global Ministries Bylaws as foundational guides in all ministry and fellowship activities and Christian living. These documents do not replace Scripture as the primary guide to Christian conduct, but rather to instruct on MC Global Ministries' approach to governing this ministry organization as a nonprofit corporation and its Chapel Fellowship community of believers.

H. After consistently attending fellowship for at least two months, potential members will be eligible to begin the process of joining the fellowship ministry team training program. Becoming a fellowship ministry team member grants a voice in fellowship ministry team member meetings and eligibility for ministry training and ministry opportunities, as well as being elected or appointed as a fellowship elder.

MC Chapel Fellowship Team Membership Process for Acceptance:

A. **Fellowship ministry team acceptance program** – Upon completion of the prerequisites and assignments, candidates will be eligible to begin training in a variety of fellowship ministry opportunities and volunteer positions. Candidates must consistently attend Sunday fellowship meeting for at least 2 months to be eligible to attend a MCCF Team Vision Class.

B. **Mentor Assignment** – During the Team Vision Class, candidates will be given a MCCF Fellowship Handbook and assigned a ministry mentor for support, guidance, and questions. After studying the fellowship handbook, candidates can take a written questionnaire and oral exam administered by the Membership Review Board.

C. **Review Board** – Membership Review Board shall be comprised of an Associate Pastor and the Board of Elders.

D. **Examination** – Candidates must subscribe to MCGM and its Chapel Fellowship statement of faith and upon passing oral and written exams, the Membership Review Board will enroll candidates as an introductory candidate to become certified as a fellowship ministry team member. Candidates will be assigned a Fellowship Elder to work with, who will help each candidate prepare for ministry in MCGM's Chapel Fellowship.

E. **Sponsorship and Acceptance** – After an approximate period of one year, the assigned Fellowship Elder can sponsor their candidate to become a certified fellowship ministry team member.

F. **Reception** – Approved candidates shall be publicly received as fellowship team members during a fellowship service and their names, addresses, and date of official acceptance shall be included in the membership record of MC Chapel Fellowship.

G. **Identification** – Approved candidates shall receive a MC Chapel Fellowship team membership identification card to be presented upon request by fellowship ushers or security personal in attending all fellowship team member meetings.

MCCF Statement of Faith

Unity between the saints in fellowship is vital. A statement of faith and fellowship principles should be stated and explained thoroughly. Those attending fellowship should be of one mind and of one heart in matters of faith and in agreement concerning worship preferences. (See Acts 1:12-14.)

The following statement of faith covers important doctrines we hold to be crucial in facilitating harmony of faith, maturity, apt discernment, and fellowship growth in the love of God.

We believe in the following—

1. In the verbal Divine inspiration of the original Scriptures.
2. In the absolute Trinity of the eternal Godhead.
3. In the deity of our Lord Jesus Christ.
4. In the personality and deity of the Holy Spirit.
5. That Satan is a real personality and controls demons and dark spiritual powers which have evil intent to do harm to mankind and all true believers in Christ.
6. In the natural depravity of humanity.
7. In the substitutionary atonement through Jesus Christ and only Jesus Christ.
8. In the propitiation for sin only by the blood of Jesus Christ.
9. In the full salvation by grace through faith in Christ and not of religious works.
10. In divine healing through atonement and prayer of faith according to God's will.
11. In the anointing of oil and prayer for the sick with confession of sin if necessary.
12. In the personal infilling of the Holy Spirit as received by the Apostles.
13. In the personal baptism of the Holy Spirit for power to minister, witness and glorify Christ.
14. In the distribution of a variety of spiritual gifts by the Holy Spirit as outlined in Scripture, as the Holy Spirit wills for those prepared in the discipline of the Lord and verified for authenticity.
15. To practice the gift of prophesy in fellowship by all trained members, to graciously reveal the secrets of the heart in ministry for one another and for newcomers or outsiders.
16. In the necessity of the new birth by the Holy Spirit.
17. In the necessity of the sanctifying work of the Holy Spirit in the believer for emotional and spiritual restoration and maturity.
18. In water baptism by immersion at an age of accountability.
19. In the one and only true Church composed of all truly born anew, blood-washed, and sanctified believers who are obedient to Christ.
20. In the evangelization of the lost within all nations of the world.
21. Public worship to be conducted with reverence, joy, thanksgiving and in orderly freedom for expressing the gifts of the Holy Spirit with discernment, decency, and order.
22. In obedience to civil government when not contrary to God's commandments.
23. In divorce only on New Testament scriptural grounds.
24. In marriage only between man and woman as husband and wife, as prescribed in the Holy Scriptures.
25. In Church government, loyalty, and obedience to those in authority over us in the Lord who practice sound doctrine based on grace, truth, and faith.
26. In the calling of individual to leadership, not as a profession, but by being taken captive by Jesus Christ and disciplined to become a true bond servant of Christ. Today, many assume and grasp leadership positions and thus seek man's approval, desire recognition and become people pleasers.

27. In tithes [21], gifts and offerings in cheerful faith with a clear conscience—without reluctance or under compulsion as God's financial plan.
28. In restitution for past wrongs whenever possible.
29. In the open table at the Lord's Supper with examination of one's heart.
30. In the free moral willpower of man, who can backslide, apostatize, and enter into judgment of the Lord.
31. In the existence of evil and unredeemable people who have seared their conscience and become reprobate (for not all have faith).
32. In demonic possession [22], co-habitation, and oppression for non-believers and believers who have yet to become cleansed and healed from past defilements, wounds to the spirit, or who suffer from a double-minded condition.
33. In the maintenance of good works and holy living through and by the Holy Spirit and God's grace and mercy.
34. In the discipline and trying work of the Lord for every believer that brings righteousness and crucifixion of the flesh.
35. In the victorious life over sin, selfishness, and bad habits through and by the Holy Spirit, the work of the cross and God's grace and mercy within the believer's life.
36. In Christian perfection (learning and doing the perfect will of God) and holiness through absolute surrender and consecration.
37. In diligent Bible study and unceasing prayer through the discipline and enabling grace of God.
38. In Christian modesty in the matter of dress, jewelry and abstaining from any appearance of evil or worldliness.
39. In the keeping of the Lord's Day as a matter of privilege rather than law with a commitment to regular assembly.
40. Regarding recreation - liberty of conscience and a godly example to the world.
41. In the immortality and conscious existence of the human soul and human spirit.
42. In the resurrection of our literal bodies, the just and the unjust.
43. In a literal heaven and life everlasting for all true and obedient believers.
44. In a final day of judgment for the incorrigibly wicked.
45. In the everlasting punishment of the un-contrite and non-repentant.
46. In the rapture of the saints or the true body of Christ at the end of the Great Tribulation.
47. In the personal, literal, bodily pre-millennia coming of Jesus Christ.
48. In a future, literal, 1,000-year reign of Christ on earth with all His saints.
49. In the Judgment Seat of Christ where the saints will finally be rewarded for their deeds of commission and omission.
50. In Christian tolerance to all denominations of the Christian faith and the invisible Universal Church of all true believers bonded in love. We desire to see unity between Christians but not at the expense of the sound teachings of our Lord Jesus Christ and godly life and character.

This statement of faith will help newcomers understand our position on crucial doctrines. These statements are neither negotiable nor changeable. Those attending must agree with the statement of faith; if not, then they should find fellowship elsewhere. Many Christians look for fellowship but always find flaws and attempt to change things to suit their perception of what the perfect fellowship should be like.

Most with this mindset are discontent with their own relationship with God. This is due to inner defilements and unbelief that drives a hidden agenda, and thus refuse to contribute to building healthy relationships: Neither do they truly serve Christ, but rather their own selfish agenda. (Romans 16:17-20).

However, asking for explanation, instruction, and scriptural confirmation to MCCF's by-laws, statement of faith and other membership documents is encouraged. Simple clarifications will usually clear up any issues of concern.

---

[21] Although tithing is an Old Testament concept under the Law, and we agree that tithing is not required under the New Covenant, the term tithe is used interchangeably with offerings in many fellowships. All giving should be in accordance with 2 Corinthians 9:6-15.

[22] Possession: Any hold which evil spirits have in or upon a person in any degree. They "possess" that which they hold. (War on the Saints, By Jesse Penn-Lewis with Evan Roberts, the 9th Edition, Thomas E. Lowe. Ltd.)

Fellowship Commitment

The fellowship of the saints requires commitment, reinforced by embracing a sincere pledge; a pledge to engage in developing a wholesome scriptural relationship with God the Father, through His Son, Jesus Christ. Each is committed to emanate a *maturing relationship* with Christ that affects their family, others in the fellowship, the body of Christ as a whole, and as a witness to the lost in the community and the world.

This commitment is not a demand by which we bind and imprison each other. This commitment is to God, giving Him permission to make us the people he desires us to be, and to allow him to incorporate us into the proper relationships that he desires for each to be in, with family, in the fellowship of the saints, and in the world. (See Ephesians 4:11-16.)

The following are scriptural standards for relationships with one another in our fellowship. One must willingly desire God's grace, mercy, and power to keep these commitments and relationship responsibilities:

A Commitment to the Lordship of Jesus Christ: I present myself to Christ, allowing his Lordship in my life to lead me, encourage me, discipline me, to use me in good works, and perfect my faith. I commit my life into his care and choose to grow up and become the person of God that he calls me to be. I commit to be diligent in learning and doing all that Christ teaches in Scripture and learn to hear and obey his voice. (See Romans 12:1-2, Luke 6:46-49.)

A Commitment to Grace: I choose to love, support, and accept you, my brothers and sisters, no matter what you say or do, what you do not say or do not do, providing your words and actions are not abusive or harmful. I will love you in whatever form you come. This love and acceptance will come from the Lord in whom I trust and call upon to work out this attitude of heart. (See Colossians 3:5-14.) This commitment to grace will include tough love in God's grace when necessary for correcting hurtful behavior, towards others or me.

A Commitment to Truth: I choose to seek and develop an honest, warm, and caring relationship with all the brethren. I will seek, in the timing of the Spirit, to deal openly and directly with you in seeking and speaking the truth concerning all challenges with my relationships—in a loving and forgiving way, so that each of you are not un-affirmed when in need, and so that any frustrations with one another may not lead to resentment or bitterness. (See Ephesians 4:25-32.)

A Commitment to Openness: I choose to open myself to you inwardly, my hurts, joys, loves, hates, hopes, disappointments, and history in wisdom and God's timing. In allowing myself to become vulnerable, I choose not to make you responsible for my own sense of well-being, happiness, or comfort. I am committed to letting you be what God has called you to be and refrain from manipulating or controlling you. (See Luke 11:37-41.)

A Commitment to Sacrifice and Prayer: Particularly, in our gatherings, but also through the week as well, I will attempt to make your needs just as important as my own as we talk, worship, and pray together. I desire to pray on a regular basis for you as God increases His grace and power in my life. I will work to be sensitive to the Holy Spirit concerning you. (See Philippians 2:1-11.)

A Commitment to Priority: I choose to put my relationship with God first with a desire to love Him with all my being and energy. Next, I choose to see my family restored to a healthy Christ-centered home, functioning in grace, love, discipline, and mercy. Following my immediate family, I choose to esteem you in fellowship in a self-sacrificing manner, desiring to see you grow in grace and knowledge of the Lord Jesus Christ and to give of my life and gifts to be part of the reason for your growth. I commit to the restoration of every fellowship family, and to foster family wholeness as well as fellowship togetherness. (See Matthew 22:37-40.)

A Commitment to Availability: I will seek to serve you with my time, energy, wisdom, finances, and material goods as God gives me grace and based on my commitment to the priority of God first, family, then fellowship. When you need my physical aid, I will attempt to be present with anything I have. (See Acts 2:43-47.)

A Commitment to Regularity: I will regard the time which our fellowship spends together weekly as time under the disciplining hand of Jesus in our midst. I choose to assist the work of the Holy Spirit in our lives by attending on a regular basis. (See Hebrews 10:19-25; Luke 9:57-62.)

A Commitment to Accountability: I give you the permission to question, confront, and challenge me in love when I seem to be failing in any aspect of my life under God, family, devotions, general spiritual growth, and the like. I trust you to be led by the Holy Spirit and be led by Christ when you do so. I need your correction and reproof so that I may fulfill my

God-given ministry amongst you. I commit to refrain from being defensive, but rather maintain an attitude of humility where we learn to care and watch out for each other in a healthy non-controlling manner. (See Ezekiel 3:16-21 & Matthew 18:12-20 Proverbs 12:1, 15; 13:1, 10, 18.)

A Commitment to Confidentiality: I realize that much of what we share would be harmful to you who shared it if it were repeated to others. Therefore, personal matters stop here. I will say nothing outside our fellowship that might be injurious or embarrassing to any one of you. (See Proverbs 10:19; 11:9, 13; 12:23; 13:3; 15:4; 18:6-8.)

A Commitment to Outreach: I choose to commit my life, by God's grace and help, to be a sacrifice through example for those outside the fellowship of our faith, in the same way that I have committed myself sacrificially for the growth and wholeness of our relationship. I will treat unbelievers exactly as if they were believers, refraining from a "better than thou attitude." I will do it in Jesus' name (not religiously) so that others are added to the Kingdom of God through God's love and by his calling. I desire my life to be an example of *a living faith emanating living water* as a testimony to those in darkness. (See Matthew 25:31-46 and John 7:38-39.)

A Commitment to Sensitivity: I choose to be sensitive and understanding to the failures of others within the fellowship. I desire to maintain an atmosphere of openness and acceptance for all, to confess sin and failure without feeling put down or condemned. I realize that many of God's children suffer from a broken or wounded spirit, and this requires time for healing. I desire to see all within the fellowship walking in the grace of God and not in the law religiously or independently in a carnal licentious manner. I choose to support those who are going through trials and the discipline of the Lord, knowing that true righteousness is achieved by God's dealings within us in everyday life. (See Galatians 6:1-5.)

A Commitment to Leadership: I choose to make a commitment to the leadership appointed in the fellowship. I recognize their responsibility to me and the congregation to be stewards who will have to give an account to the Lord. I commit myself to honesty by sharing my true feelings with leadership and refrain from saying what I think they would want to hear. I choose to discuss any problems that I may have toward leadership with that leader or leaders in private. I choose not to gossip, malign, slander or criticize leaders behind their backs. If I have an irreconcilable difference with leadership and fellowship doctrine, then I will choose to fellowship elsewhere since this would better for my spiritual growth and not cause discord among the brethren. If a leader is caught in an open sin, I choose to confront him—if he or she has not already been confronted. I choose to hold him or her accountable until proper discipline has been exercised and the rest of the leadership restores that person. I will refrain from gossip but choose to see such falling from grace to be openly dealt with before the congregation. (See Hebrews 13:7, 17.)

A Commitment to Ministry Support: I choose to commit to give in financial support for valid ministry needs, not reluctantly or under pressure or compulsively, but as I have determined in my mind cheerfully. I choose to give out of my reasonable ability, not with the motive to get something in return. However, God does provide in abundance for every good work. The Lord has said, *"Give and it shall be given unto you."* (See Luke 6:38; 2 Corinthians 9:6-15; 1 Corinthians 9:1-18; 1 Timothy 6:17-19; Philippians 4:10-20.)

A Commitment to Order and Discernment: I choose to adhere to common courtesy and decent order within all meetings. I choose to practice my gifting(s) not to gain attention but rather for the encouragement, uplifting, and edification of our body of believers, with sensitivity to visitors, newcomers, or outsiders. I choose to seek from the Lord, wisdom, and discernment and to test the spiritual experiences shared by my brothers and sisters, as well as my own. I choose to seek from leadership the authority to practice my giftings in meetings. I will accept direction and instruction in the practice any spiritual gift and refrain from speaking in an unknown tongue out loud to edify myself, but rather speak in a tongue silently and pledge to confer with leadership to see if my gift of tongues is of the Holy Spirit and not counterfeit or carnal. [23] (See 1 Corinthians 12:1 - 14:33.)

---

[23] False Giftings and Carnal Spiritualism: Most churches and fellowship that believe the gifts of the Holy Spirit are to be practiced have ignorantly become deceived by counterfeiting spirits and teachings that promote carnal spiritualism. Carnal spiritualism primarily invades fellowship through the practice of speaking in an unknown tongue through one's own personal spirit. This type of spiritualism opens the door to counterfeiting demons that produce false gifts, such as divination disguised as prophesy. Many succumb to false manifestations that produce spiritual-emotional euphoria that is much more than self-edifying, but rather self-indulgent, entertaining, and distracting—drawing attention to self, rather than glorifying Christ.

Fellowship Agreement

I understand and agree with the written Statement of Faith and Fellowship Commitment:

I agree that if I fall out of agreement with MC Chapel Fellowship Statement of Faith and Fellowship Commitment or the fellowship's governing rules, that I will not attempt to undermine said documents by verbal dissent among the brethren but will express my disagreement in writing to the leadership of this fellowship.

I understand and agree that if I stand in opposition to the fellowship's Statement of Faith, Fellowship Commitment, and its governing bylaws, and become unable to accept these differences—and verbally oppose or undermine said statements—leadership of this fellowship will exercise their duties in banning me from fellowship until I have reconciled my differences and refrain from verbally challenging or undermining the aforementioned statements, beliefs, and bylaws.

I understand and agree that all reports of felonious activity, child abuse, or domestic violence will be reported to the proper authorities as soon as possible.

I understand and agree that any expressed contemplation of suicide by those in attendance in this fellowship will be reported to the proper authorities as soon as possible.

I understand and agree that the leadership will ban anyone who has been convicted of any pedophilia offense from attending functions or meetings where children are or can be present.

I understand and agree that it is the policy of this fellowship that if a person attending refuses to renounce sinful alliances and or a perverse lifestyle, including homosexuality or any other sinful works of the flesh, that person will be subjected to fellowship censure (shunned) and banned from attending fellowship. (See Galatians 5:13-26, 1 Corinthians 5:1-13.)

I understand and agree that fellowship meetings may from time to time be held in a private home that is not open to the public. The host, leader, or pastor holding meetings in a private home setting has the right to cancel or discontinue all meetings in such a venue without explanation and without notification. My attendance in home meetings will be respectful of privacy, meeting times and schedules, and maintain a friendly attitude.

Leadership and designated representatives have the right to remove any person(s) who attends a fellowship meeting if they behave in a disorderly manner, demonstrate intoxication, or threatening behavior, interrupting, or disrupting the meeting(s).

I understand and agree that fellowship meetings may not provide infant or childcare. If such facilities are available, an equitable system of childcare will be the responsibility of the leadership or those designated in conjunction with all who attend, including parents of children. Leadership may require signed waivers of parents whose children are cared for within the fellowship or a home fellowship during any meetings where childcare is available, as well as implement a child identification system.

The above fellowship commitment will require your signature along with the fellowship disclaimer stated herein. Both documents will be provided to you when you chose to become a MC Chapel Fellowship team member.

Fellowship Disclaimer

The following explains why each member is to sign a fellowship disclaimer. A disclaimer is a document that lays out what an organization or individual is not responsible for. The following is a copy of our fellowship and ministry disclaimer:

- I understand that MC Global Ministries and its Chapel Fellowship is a Christian religious organization and as such, is a not-for-profit corporation funded by donations and offerings. Its resources, such as books, literature, workshops, and classes are offered on a donation or honorarium basis to help individuals develop a close relationship with God our heavenly Father, through his son Jesus Christ. MCGM and MCCF and its leadership do not guarantee an individual's success in this endeavor nor promise anyone will be blessed by participating, contributing, or donating financially to this fellowship and its work.

- We defer completely to the promises of God in Christ Jesus, as Scripture teaches: *"For the Son of God, Jesus Christ, whom we preached among you, Silvanus and Timothy and I, was not Yes and No; but in him it is always Yes. For all the promises of God find their Yes in him. That is why we utter the Amen through him, to the glory of God. But it is God who establishes us with you in Christ, and has commissioned us; he has put his seal upon us and given us his Spirit in our hearts as a guarantee"* (2 Corinthians 1:19-22).

- It is up to everyone by exercising his or her own faith in God through Christ that will establish maturity in Christ for each individual, then collectively as a fellowship. The key is becoming Christlike and thus become established in Christ, abiding in him continually.

- MCGM and MCCF's leadership refrains from making those coming to fellowship dependent on leadership's faith and ministry, acting as a go-between for God. Jesus Christ is to be everyone's intermediary between them and our heavenly Father: *"For there is one God, and there is one mediator between God and men, the man Christ Jesus, who gave himself as a ransom for all, which is the testimony given at the proper time"* (1 Timothy 2:5-7).

- Your success is dependent on your own desire, determination, decisions, obedience, and dedication (faith) to the person of Jesus Christ, his Gospel and obtaining God's seal and guarantee by receiving and the continual infilling of the Holy Spirit.

- Every saint in fellowship, from the congregant to those who serve in leadership, are to learn how to, *"Work out your own salvation with fear and trembling, for it is God who works in you, both to will and to work for his good pleasure"* (Philippians 2:12-13).

- For every believer in Christ attending MCCF, a Biblical standard of morality is expected to be practiced. Anyone attending who strays from these Biblical moral standards or attempts to sway others to practice immorality, sexual perversion, or criminal behavior will not be tolerated and if lacking repentance that bears fruit, such persons will suffer excommunication. The Apostle Paul instructs the following: *"I wrote to you in my letter not to associate with sexually immoral people—not at all meaning the sexually immoral of this world, or the greedy and swindlers, or idolaters, since then you would need to go out of the world. But now I am writing to you not to associate with anyone who bears the name of brother if he is guilty of sexual immorality or greed, or is an idolater, reviler, drunkard, or swindler—not even to eat with such a one. For what have I to do with judging outsiders? Is it not those inside the church whom you are to judge? God judges those outside. "Purge the evil person from among you."* (1 Corinthians 5:9-13).

- We refrain from judging or pointing the finger at the sexually immoral of this world, whether heterosexual or LGBTQ (Lesbian, Gay, Bisexual, Transgender and Queer community). However, we do not accept anyone to be a team member, or allow such to become member of this fellowship, who call themselves a Christian (a believer in Christ) and believe they are morally sound and at the same time practice wickedness, we therefore do not associate or fellowship with anyone who bears the name of brother if he is guilty of sexual immorality or greed, or is an idolater, reviler, drunkard, or swindler—not even to eat with such a one.

Fellowship Security, Domestic Violence, and Active Threat Protocols

In these dark days, fellowship safety and security should be a primary concern for every church nationwide. It is no longer just the false Christian wolf that emotionally and spiritually preys on victims. Pedophiles, sexual predators, and mentally deranged people make their way into fellowship meetings to victimize the innocent. What is extremely alarming is the increased mass shooting attacks on fellowship meetings throughout America.

MCGM and MCCF employs active threat protocols in the case of physical assault against our fellowship during meetings, worship, and Sunday fellowship.

Most potential threats to churches stem from domestic violence where a targeted family member is attending fellowship. If you are experiencing domestic issues where possessive, aggressive, combative, or controlling behavior manifests, you have an obligation to inform the MCCF ministry staff. All reports of such issues are held in confidentiality.

In reporting and seeking counsel you will help yourself and your family become connected to our fellowship support network and learn about community support and resources. Our security staff incorporates appropriate safety and threat awareness protocols on a case-by-case basis.

If there is an aggressor or intruder meaning harm to our fellowship members, individually or to the fellowship during meetings, we have various plans of action to heighten the necessary steps for safety awareness, prevention, and action against potential threats.

Training for worst case scenarios is part of the security staff's objectives as well as training those attending fellowship in the case of active physical threats: *Threats such as an active shooter or an enraged person wielding a knife, bomb threats, or other types of assaults.*

We do not disclose the identity of our security staff, or our procedures used by our trained security team. However, all who attend our fellowship meetings can expect training and emergency practice drills, as well as instructions on safety (personal and group) at varied times throughout the year.

A note on firearms: We post signs indicating that our fellowship facility is a weapon free zone and that we have plain clothed armed security team in place and 24-hour surveillance. Open carry and concealed carry are not allowed on the grounds or in any meeting.

However, for concealed carry permit holders, please refrain from brining your weapon to any fellowship meeting until you are vetted and trained by our security team in our safety and active threat protocols.

MCCF Ministries and Meeting Expectations

The following is an overview of MC Chapel Fellowship's ministries, each with a brief description. These ministries are reviewed by the MCGM's founding Board of Directors and ministry team leaders, along with input from the fellowship team members, and as such are subject to change for improvement to meet ministerial needs, productivity (fruit), and for administrative efficiency.

Each fellowship meeting, class, or workshop will have a different objective(s) and varied approaches in accomplishing those objectives. Meetings are governed by the leader or speaker and are to be held and maintained in good order with the understanding that the Holy Spirit and the Spirit of Christ are given leadership credence with discernment, by the leader, speaker, or facilitator.

It is a common practice and expectation within a wide variety of fellowships and denominations that meetings be given over to the supposed anointing where spiritualism and counterfeit manifestations take control of a meeting sporadically, randomly, and usually through certain ritualistic routines (in the name of the manifestation of the Holy Spirit). In truth, most of the time this practice undermines the work of the Holy Spirit (the Spirit of Truth) and short circuits the successful expounding of sound doctrine. The proper expounding of Scripture is derived from a deeper understanding of the Word of God. Therefore, decency and order in all MCCF meetings will be maintained.

Interrupting speakers during their presentation is not condoned, whether it be a confirming or approving comment that draws attention to the one speaking out of turn, or a question asked during a non-question and answer period. MCCF normally incorporates in every meeting for questions, comments, dissent, or disagreement.

If dissent is expressed in a contentious manner, with intent to undermine order and cause dissension or difficulties—that person will be corrected. If the disruptive behavior continues, that person will be escorted from the meeting and barred from attending all future meetings. They can return to fellowship after they have demonstrated fruit of repentance, resolved any misunderstandings, and become aligned with MCCF doctrine.

The following are MCCF current and future core meetings:
(Days of the week and times are subject to change.)

<u>Sunday Prayer and Fellowship:</u>

- **Prayer and Solemn Assembly:** From 9:45 a.m. to 10:30 a.m. prayer is held in a designated meeting room—for prayer that is heartfelt, sincere, and fervent. A quiet atmosphere is maintained during this time where prayers are offered. This time of prayer is a solemn gathering for individuals to pray, or small groups can be formed where praying in agreement is facilitated. One of the staff ministers will also be available for prayer requests and act as a moderator.

- **Worship and Fellowship:** From 10:40 a.m. the sanctuary is open for personal greeting, singing (worship), sharing prophesy or current issues, and announcements. The fellowship message normally begins at 11:15 a.m. and usually lasts thirty to forty-five minutes. We urge everyone to arrive at Sunday meetings on time (preferably by 9:35 a.m. for solemn prayer and 10:30 a.m. for fellowship, worship, and message).

Monday Evening Recovery Group: 7:00 p.m. (Future Meeting)

- **Recovery Through Christ,** is not a step program, but rather a confidential recovery meeting based on God's recovery program founded in Biblical principles and the Holy Spirit's work in healing for those suffering from a wounded spirit and damaged emotions. The text used is: **Crushed in Spirit 2nd Edition** *Help for Christians suffering from a wounded and broken spirit* ISBN 978-1-943412-16-7

Tuesday Evening Equip for Ministry Class: 7:00 p.m. (Future Meeting)

- **Equipped for Life and Ministry in the Last Days** is a practical class that is designed to help those attending become prepared to navigate successfully through the coming persecution and troubles leading up to the rapture and Christ's second coming. The text used is: **Equipped for Life and Ministry in the Last Days** *Biblical Principles to help Endure and Minister during the Final Awakening* ISBN 978-1-943412-13-6.

- **What We Believe and Why** instruction will also be incorporated into this Tuesday evening class, using this fellowship handbook.

Wednesday Evening Home Bible Study: 7:00 p.m. (Future Meeting)

- **Fellowship and Lessons,** these mid-week meetings are held in the homes of our Bible study leaders. Home Bible Study meetings are tailored to discuss important doctrinal issues and challenges facing God's people in this hour. In attending you will have the opportunity to ask questions and comment while attending a specific Home Bible Study group of your choosing. Each Home Bible Study group will have different themes and subjects related Scripture and Doctrine founded in the word of God. A variety of studies will be offered, and when finished with one study, an attendee can rotate to another Home Bible Study group and so on.

Thursday Evening Broadcast (open to the public): 7:00 p.m. (Future Ministry)

- **Midnight Cry Awakening Broadcast,** a live Internet broadcast moderated by one of our ministry leaders will have special quests, and guided in a round table discussion on topics such as; last days discernment, true revival, persecution, personal safety and security, becoming ready, sound doctrine versus false teachings, and much more. This broadcast will be held in the fellowship sanctuary and will be open to audience who are fellowship members only, by way of request.

Workshops and Training Classes

Our Lord commissioned his disciples to teach and train others to become his disciples. Unfortunately, we find that through the centuries each generation of believers have fallen short in their efforts to make disciples of Christ—God's way.

There have been times throughout these centuries where the body of Christ has truly shined, having a core of true disciples serving Christ. However, in these last days true discipleship training is almost non-existent, as most Christians today merely follow Christ's name and avoid submitting to Christ's lordship, training, and discipline.

When God has mature disciples to work with, then from that foundation of maturity they are to walk in "good works" as directed by the Holy Spirit. *"For we are his workmanship, created in Christ Jesus for good works, which God prepared beforehand, that we should walk in them"* (Ephesians 2:10).

MCCF's mission is to make followers of Christ into sincere and genuine disciples of Christ who become mature. Then in turn, the Holy Spirit can begin to draw and add new converts to a fellowship of mature believers and bring back into the fold the disenfranchised or wounded Christian who left formal fellowship or church for various reasons.

As an outreach to the frustrated believer and for those in our ranks, we offer workshops where we concentrate on presenting sound teachings that are practical. The workshop format and small class structure gives each attendee opportunity to interact with the teacher with questions and comments.

Most of our workshops are held on Saturday mid-morning to mid-afternoon with larger seminars and conferences conducted over two to four days. Many of those teaching or facilitating a workshop or class will also train others to become qualified to teach in a practical manner.

Another mission concerning these workshops and classes is to restore sound and practical life changing theology to those who have an ear to hear. It is our desire to see God have Christian workers in his service who are equipped to minister the Gospel to a lost generation. Many are called to teach and mentor but were never given opportunity to learn how to mentor or how to minister effectively.

Counseling and Prayer-Support-Group

MCCF offers pastoral counseling, mentoring, and support for troubled and wounded Christians. Many Christians struggle after they are born again due to the hidden and unresolved wounds from past trauma. MCI Recovery Ministries (a separate 501 (c) 3 organization) is founded on Scripture and Biblical principles that the Holy Spirit will use in healing a wounded spirit and a broken heart. We bring our own recovery, training, gifting, and the Spirit of Christ to each counselee to aid in healing and recovery. *"The Lord is near to the brokenhearted and saves the crushed in spirit"* (Psalm 34:18). (This is a future ministry.)

Trauma: James 3:6 speaks of trauma caused by perverse words and abusive actions towards another person. *"The tongue is set among our members, staining the whole body, setting on fire the entire course of life, and set on fire by hell."* Proverbs 15:4 states: *"A gentle tongue is a tree of life, but perverseness breaks the spirit."* Many suffer from childhood trauma and other abuses and do not realize past trauma is the main cause for a troubled life as a Christian adult.

Burden Bearing: Mature and trained Christians are called to fulfill the law of Christ which is bearing the burden of others who are struggling. *"Bear one another's burdens, and so fulfill the law of Christ"* (Galatians 6:2). Bearing each other's burdens is vital in giving Christ opportunity to heal wounded and troubled Christians.

Intensive Care: Unresolved issues of heart and spirit have upsetting symptoms and can carry intense emotional pain when they emerge from hiding. Care and support from trained counselors, support group work, and the comfort of the Holy Spirit becomes vital during this aspect of the healing process. *"The purpose in a man's mind is like deep water, but a man of understanding will draw it out"* (Proverbs 20:5).

The Gifts of the Holy Spirit: Without the Holy Spirit leading and facilitating healing and recovery— attempts in becoming whole fall short. We are admonished to employ the gifts of the Holy Spirit with wisdom in facilitating Christ centered healing and recovery. The gift of prophesy is used routinely in counseling within God's timing to expose secret or hidden issues of the heart and spirit. (See 1 Corinthians 14:24-25.) The counselee's own spirit working with the Holy Spirit, if understood and applied properly, will reveal the root issues, and facilitate resolution. *"The spirit of man is the lamp of the Lord, searching all his innermost parts"* (Proverbs 20:27).

The following is the main portion or our counseling disclaimer. We stress that each counselee and each ministry worker and mentor understand the limitations and restraints to MCCF's healing and recovery ministry.

Counseling Disclaimer

I understand that Message of the Cross Chapel Fellowship (MCCF) and MCI Recovery Ministries are under the direction of Message of the Cross Global Ministries (MCGM), both being non-profit ministries that provides pastoral counseling and mentoring based on Biblical principles and operates on a cost recovery basis only. No fee for counseling is charged, however a financial honorarium (donation) is appreciated with each session or meeting.

I also acknowledge that MCCF/MCI Recovery Ministries' counselors and pastors are not licensed mental health professionals or medical practitioners. As such, I further state that I have sought counseling and/or mentoring on my own initiative. I am under no obligation to accept or reject any of the counsel that I may receive from MCCF/ MCI Recovery Ministries pastoral counseling and mentoring ministries.

If symptoms of mental anxiety or emotional distress become overwhelming, I accept responsibility to seek professional help through a qualified mental health referral agency or by recommendation from a licensed medical practitioner (family doctor) and to notify my MCCF/ MCI Recovery Ministries counselor as soon as possible.

I also acknowledge that any clear self-harm threat that is spoken or written that is heard by or discovered by a MCCF/ MCI Recovery Ministries counselor, notification to authorities will be exercised by that MCCF/ MCI Recovery Ministries counselor as soon as possible.

Further, I acknowledge that memories of past trauma are very apt to surface spontaneously during, after counseling, or during a support group meeting that may implicate abuse by people from my past. A memory of a parent, sibling, aunt or uncle, babysitter or neighbor may emerge. If this is the case, the decisions taken by myself concerning these memories—both legally and in exercising relationship accountability will be my responsibility. It is my responsibility to decide whether to seek legal counsel and advice as well as seek consultation from a licensed mental health referral agency or a licensed medical practitioner.

MCCF/ MCI Recovery Ministries counselor or counselee can discontinue counseling/mentoring/support group participation at any time without reason. Notice of such discontinuation by either is requested if feasible.

Prayer, Spiritual Warfare, Deliverance, Discovering Ground and Resistance

The effectual fervent prayer of the righteous, praying in agreement is the cornerstone of our fellowship and ministerial works. Ministry leadership teaches the importance of Holy Spirit led prayer and intercession. Without genuine prayer we will fall back into carnal living instead of the abundant life in God, where He intervenes, and we are led by the Holy Spirit, delivered from the evil one, and protected by God.

The Apostle Paul penned the importance of prayer with the following passage, *"For we do not want you to be unaware, brothers, of the affliction we experienced in Asia. For we were so utterly burdened beyond our strength that we despaired of life itself. Indeed, we felt that we had received the sentence of death. But that was to make us rely not on ourselves but on God who raises the dead. He delivered us from such a deadly peril, and he will deliver us. On him we have set our hope that he will deliver us again. You also must help us by prayer, so that many will give thanks on our behalf for the blessing granted us through the prayers of many"* (2 Corinthians 1:8-11).

When the Apostle Peter was arrested by Herod and plans were made to execute Peter in order to please the Jews, the account in the book of Acts reads, *"So Peter was kept in prison; but earnest prayer was made to God by the church"* (Acts 12:5). Those earnest prayers moved God to send an angel of Lord to deliver Peter—miraculously!

This is our main emphasis—prayer, not just lip service, but meaningful and earnest prayer by the fellowship of the saints. As you become familiar and ready, you are welcome to take part in the ministry prayer team by participating in our prayer meetings in designated homes, or our Saturday meetings. Each attendee is welcome to participate in our Sunday morning Prayer and Solemn Assembly time (9:45 a.m. to 10:30 a.m.).

Spiritual Warfare and deliverance from demonic oppression, possession and cohabitation are important to understand, with sound instruction that is Scripturally accurate. The most important aspect in dealing the dark forces of hell and Satan is that Christians who engage in spiritual combat actively deal with their own issues of heart and spirit.

Many Christians suffer from the demonic because they still have "ground" within them—ground meaning defilements, impurities, and unbelief. *"Since we have these promises, beloved, let us cleanse ourselves from every defilement of body and spirit, bringing holiness to completion in the fear of God"* (2 Corinthians 7:1). Also: *"Submit yourselves therefore to God. Resist the devil, and he will flee from you. Draw near to God, and he will draw near to you. Cleanse your hands, you sinners, and purify your hearts, you double-minded. Be wretched and mourn and weep."* (James 4:7-8).

Missions—Local and Foreign

MCCF's primary mission is to bring the Gospel of Christ in an uncompromised manner to those who are serious about submitting to the lordship of Christ. Wounded and disenfranchised believers in Christ are everywhere, in our community and throughout the region. It is these and the lost that we desire to reach. It is the wounded, hurting, and the troubled as well as the sinner who wants deliverance from the bondage of sin, *"And as he sat at table in the house, behold, many tax collectors and sinners came and sat down with Jesus and his disciples. And when the Pharisees saw this, they said to his disciples, 'Why does your teacher eat with tax collectors and sinners?' But when he heard it, he said, 'Those who are well have no need of a physician, but those who are sick. Go and learn what this means, 'I desire mercy, and not sacrifice.' For I came not to call the righteous, but sinners"* (Matthew 9:10-13).

Local Missions: As part of our local outreach, we are supporting MCI Recovery Ministries' Jump Start Program (future ministry). Updates of this local mission will be presented to the fellowship for donations and volunteer. Future plans for a homeless shelter, day center, temporary and short-term shelter and in-depth recovery are under development.

Foreign Missions: We support two foreign missions, ✞Pastor Gideon Mudenyo and his wife Evelyn have been in our prayers and financial support since 2003. Pastor Gideon and his family live and minister in Webuye, Kenya East Africa. ✞ Pastor Dave Tecson in the Philippines, he with his wife and family minister to the indigenous Filipinos with the Gospel as true bond servants of Christ. Both our missionary brothers are native of their prospective countries, raised up by the Lord to minister to those in their own country. Pastor Gideon has traveled here twice to visit and effectively expound and teach God's word. We are planning to bring Pastor Dave here also when funds are available.

Resource Library

We are developing an extensive resource library of books, booklets, literature, and DVD available to check out or to obtain by donation. Review the ministry's online message archive page at: www.mcgmin.com

Ministry Websites

MC Global Ministries: www.mcgmin.com (Main ministry website.)

Leadership Structure

Charles Pretlow, Senior Pastor: It was in 1973, when Charles accepted Christ, just after his reenlistment in the Marines. Then in 1974, after reading David Wilkerson's book The Vision, he accepted Christ's call to full time ministry, and requested an early release from the Corps. Miraculously, his honorable discharge was granted.

In January of 1975 he began Bible College and accepted his first ministry appointment. His years of formal education includes a Bachelor of Science in Business Administration and years of leadership training in the military, as a coach, and in pastoral counseling and mentoring has helped him in ministry. However, his more in-depth training, wisdom, and character development was honed through years of ministering in a wilderness type training, facilitated by the Lord's discipline and training. His call is helping Christians become able to endure to the end of the Great Tribulation. Most Christians are not prepared for the coming troubles that God will use to make His church "without spot or blemish" —if you will, to become rapture ready.

Mark Otto, Associate Pastor: Years of ministry, leadership, mentoring and counseling experience, along with the gifts of the Spirit has proven Mark is very effective in helping others work through the most difficult challenges.

Like all the founding directors, Mark can empathize with those challenges in becoming whole in Christ. Mark's ability and gifting to instruct and exhort from the word of God is insightful, challenging and uplifting; in patience he can explain the harder teachings of Christ and Scripture. Mark shares the preaching and teaching aspects of MC Chapel Fellowship along with mentoring others in fellowship to become mature disciples of Christ.

His technical background lends well to handling the broadcast and production aspects of MCGM ministries teachings and Chapel Fellowship services.

MC Global Ministries Governing Board of Directors and Future Ministry Leaders

MCCF is governed by MC Global Ministries founding board of directors. A list of the founding board of directors is available upon request. A separate document is also available listing name and contact information for all ministry and home group leaders.

Hundreds Listen to our Messages Online

From Texas to Canada and from Kenya to Australia dozens support this work and stay encouraged and strengthened by listening or viewing our archived message stored on the Internet. Some are preparing to represent this work full time when the Lord releases additional MCGM training centers modeled after M C Chapel Fellowship here in Canon City, Colorado.

Recommended Bible Translations

We recommend a quality word-for-word translation such as the American Standard, Revised Standard, or English Standard versions. (You might want to use several translations as well several Bible dictionaries and a concordance.) Stay away from what we term *designer Bibles* written by some of the popular but errant teachers who add their commentary to reinforce their false doctrine. They do not change canon text, but in their notes and study guide they add their slant and false interpretations.[24] This approach is a powerful tool for the devil to elevate wayward teachings and wrong interpretation to an almost equal stature to the Word of God. When a naïve or gullible believer reads Scripture using a designer Bible, the subliminal effect upon an impressible reader often equates the author's notes and interpretation to that of Scripture.

Contact Information

MC Global Ministries
www.mcgmin.com (833) 695 -1236
Hours of Operation: 9 AM to 4:30 PM M – F

MC Chapel Fellowship
Sunday Fellowship Meeting Times:
Intercessory Prayer Meeting: 9:30 AM to 10:30 AM
Fellowship and Worship: 10:45 AM
Administration Hours: Monday - Thursday 9AM to 4:30 PM
Wilderness Voice Publishing
Administration Hours: 9AM to 4:30 PM M - F
Mailing Address for All Operations:
PO Box 857 - Canon City, Colorado 81215

Senior Pastor Charles Pretlow: (833) 695-1236 Ext. 11
Pastor Mark Otto: (833) 695-1236 Ext. 12

---

[24] Scofield Reference Bible was the first Bible published to popularize man's interpretation of the Word of God in note form side by side Scripture. Cyrus I. Scofield first published his work in 1909 and systematically interwove his own interpretation of Scripture in his notes. Scofield's work proved to be the source of the false doctrine of the pre-tribulation rapture. Scofield's notes on the Book of Revelation are a major source for the various timetables, judgments, and plagues elaborated by Hal Lindsey and Tim LaHaye, who also promote this same error.

Class Notes

We recommend taking notes and asking questions during your formal instruction on becoming a MCCF fellowship team member.

_____

_____

_____

_____

_____

_____

_____

_____

_____

_____

_____

_____

_____

_____

_____

_____

_____

_____

_____

_____

_____

_____

_____

_____

_____

_____

_____

_____

_____